Who's Really In Control

JESSICA GREEN

Kingdom
Ministry Publications
877-286-6372
www.kingdomgroup.net

Scripture quotations are taken from the Holy Bible, New International Version®. Copyright 1985 by The Zondervan Corporation.

Who's Really in Control
ISBN 978-0-9823390-1-5
Copyright © 2010 Jessica Green

Published by Kingdom Ministry Publications
Kingdom Come International
2495 Cedar St. Suite 8-b • Holt, MI 48842

Cover by Wake Design Group
info@wakedesigngroup.com

Kingdom
Ministry Publications
877-286-6372
www.kingdomgroup.net

CONTENTS

Artist, Angelique Ritchie

It may appear there is no one on the throne, thus begging the question "who is in control?" Never forget however, the Lion of the Tribe of Judah is ever present waiting to be invited into your life and willing to take control of whatever you are willing to let go of.

DEDICATION

First, I want to dedicate this book to my family. Each and every one has played individual roles in shaping and influencing my life. I love all of you for it.

Second, I'd like to dedicate this book to my spiritual parents, Pastors Mark and Linda Cowart, for maturing me in the Word of God. Your perfect mix of humbleness, humor, and willingness to share your own life experiences helped to truly make the Word of God come to life. Thank you so much.

Finally, I would like to dedicate this book to my sister, Teresa Louis Hilburn, who passed away on November 2nd, 2007, at the young age of 34. I pray that God will take your death and turn it into something that brings Him glory. (Her death is a prime example of what this book is about; how our choices in life dictate our blessings or curses.) I love you Teresa, and I'll see you when my work on earth is done or at the rapture, whichever comes first.

INTRODUCTION

What is this book all about, you ask? It's about exposing Satan's lie and obtaining our God-given blessings! This lie from Satan is that everything that happens is for a reason; meaning life is just a great big chess game, God and Satan are the opponents, and we are the chess pieces.

However, if every move in life is planned by God, then Satan really isn't an opponent but rather just another chess piece. I assure you Satan has a will of his own just as you and I do and God is not playing a board game with His creation.

God wants a personal relationship with His creation based on love and trust (faith), just as our parents did with us and we do with our children. It's through this relationship that we obtain blessings in life. Without this relationship we are vulnerable to the enemy, Satan.

There are two classes of people on this earth: 1) Those who have accepted Jesus Christ as their Lord and Savior; and 2) Those who have rejected Jesus. Satan knows he already owns the second category of people, so he must somehow reach the first category. The Bible calls these people "Christians" and "the church."

Since Satan knows he cannot get rid of the church, his plan

is to bring lies and confusion into it until the church is no longer a threat. We are no longer a threat if we're doing nothing at all because we believe God's in control of everything and we're simply waiting on Him; nor are we a threat if we simply "practice religion" but have no personal relationship with God. When the church is full of religion, it sacrifices relationship, both with God and with one another.

You may be asking yourself right now, what then is religion? Maybe you thought "religion" just means that you believe in God. That's part of it, but Satan has helped to turn religion into the practice of laws and rituals in connection with your belief system. When church becomes more about laws and rituals than exhibiting the love of God, then that church is operating under a religious spirit.

It's not always the church staff itself but sometimes it's a member of the congregation operating under a religious spirit. Someone exhibiting a religious spirit does two things: 1) They show more concern for the rules and regulations; and 2) They bring attention to themselves rather than God.

This is what is meant by the letter of the law versus the spirit of the law. The letter of the law is practicing religion. The spirit of the law is when you keep the love of God in your heart. Paul explains this in 2 Corinthians, which is a book of the Bible I highly recommend you read. He states in 2 Corinthians 3:6—

> . . . *not of the letter but of the Spirit; for the letter kills, but the Spirit gives life.*

In the Book of Isaiah, the first chapter, we read that the Israelites, God's chosen people, had become wicked, yet they still practiced all the religious rituals God had instructed them to do (e.g., sacrifices, offerings, assembling together in worship, etc.). However, God says in Isaiah 1:13—

> *Stop bringing meaningless offerings! Your incense is detestable to me. New Moons, Sabbaths and convocations—I cannot bear your evil assemblies.*

They were practicing religion but void of any real relationship with God. God is not interested in our rituals, He's interested in our heartfelt worship. Can you imagine God showing up one Sunday morning at your church and saying, "Stop all this racket; songs that you don't mean a word of, reciting My Word and not having a clue what it means, prayers that are just spoken from the lips but not from the heart. I cannot bear your evil assemblies." Wow, my insides shudder just writing that.

Religion as we see it today, in my opinion, is a false relationship. It's actually a relationship with yourself rather than with your creator. Religious people are what I like to call WIIFMITES (What's In It For Me?)

So what is God looking for then in a Christian? James 1:27 reads —

> *Religion that God our Father accepts as pure and faultless is this: to look after orphans and widows in their distress and to keep oneself from being polluted by the world.*

People generally feel better about themselves by being involved in religious activity (going to church, etc.), but if they're not living for God in reality, they're forfeiting their blessings. They attend church on special holidays or give a little money to charities from time to time in order to satisfy their religious obligation.

Satan loves this form of religion. He will even encourage people to attend church on special holidays or to give a little money here or a little there. Why? Going to church does not make you righteous nor will it save you, but if attending once in a while appeases the religious spirit within you, without the true relationship with Jesus Christ, then Satan knows he can keep you from your true destiny.

What is your true destiny? Jeremiah 29:11 says —

> *"For I know the plans I have for you," declares the Lord, "plans to prosper you and not to harm you, plans to give you hope and a future."*

So your true destiny is a long, healthy, and prosperous life. How does Satan keep you from this destiny? By you believing his lies and practicing religion rather than acting on God's truth. One of the most destructive lies Satan has infiltrated the church with is: "Don't worry, God's in control."

How many times have you heard someone say, "Don't worry about that situation, just give it to God because He's in control." At funerals we hear, "The Good Lord gives and the Good Lord takes away." "God must have needed so-and-so in heaven because He took him from us." "I don't understand why that happened in so-and-so's life but God knows what He's doing." I could go on and on with such comments that we've all heard and some of us have probably even spoken ourselves.

Why then, if God is in control, are there so many who lack money, food, health, and so forth? Who's responsible for that? Should I blame God when I don't have enough money for gas or groceries? Should I blame Satan? After all, the Word says the thief comes to steal, kill, and destroy; and Satan is the supreme thief.

Plus we know what the thief's intention is according to John 10:10—

The thief comes only to steal and kill and destroy; I have come that they may have life, and have it to the full.

I hope to show you in this book how we've allowed Satan to rob many of us from our rightful blessings with this lie out of the pit of hell. Christians and non-Christians alike have been hurt by this lie. Christians sit back and wait for God to move on their behalf rather than seek God's direction on what they need to be doing themselves, or they just accept the negative in their lives as a plan from God and therefore miss out on so many blessing opportunities.

Non-Christians see the destruction of the sinful nature around them and believe either God is responsible for making it happen or is to blame for not stopping it and therefore refuse to serve such a God. I believe this is the more tragic result of Satan's lie. It drags more people to hell because they can't understand how a "loving God allows such things to happen."

Many pastors teach that God created each person just the way they are and that He did so with a purpose and plan in mind. If that's the case, why then when a child is born with a deformity or abnormality do Christians pray for a healing? If there's a medical procedure that can correct the deformity or abnormality, why do we opt for that procedure rather than just accept what God created? If you believe we are created just the way God wanted us, then you must believe He created that person with that deformity or abnormality. In that case, how dare you then suggest that He made a mistake and ask Him to correct it!

If we become sick or diseased, why do we turn to God and ask Him to take it away if everything happens for a reason within God's control? If He made us just the way we are, maybe that sickness or disease is part of our design. And if these sicknesses are of God, then why did Jesus heal people while here on earth and tell us to go and heal the sick as well? Wouldn't Jesus have been working against God and telling us to do the same if this were the case?

Sicknesses, diseases, and deformities were never part of God's plan. I believe Adam and Eve were created with perfect DNA. There were no such things in existence as diseases, viruses, or deformities until sin entered the world. I believe the sin nature that entered this world through Adam and Eve's sin is responsible for altering man's DNA which allows for sicknesses, diseases, and deformities.

I also believe natural things such as drugs, alcohol, and improper eating habits alter our DNA which opens the door for sicknesses to enter our bodies. Why then if we partake of these things do we blame God when our children are not born perfect or we or a loved one becomes sick?

Then there's always the enemy whispering to us, suggesting that we have contracted a sickness or disease which, if we entertain that thought long enough and accept it, we will end up with it.

If someone came to you with a contract to sell you an ink pen for $10,000, you would not sign that contract. As a matter of fact, if you were wise you would destroy that contract. We need to be wise enough to do the same with the enemy; destroy the thought of any contracted sickness or disease!

As a born again Christian, we have authority over the sin nature, and we need to start exercising that authority.

Yes, God LOVES us just the way we are, but that doesn't mean He MADE us just the way we are.

Can God use someone who was born less than perfect to reach others with the Gospel? Yes, He can. Can God take an event in someone's life such as being cured of cancer and use that testimony to reach millions? Absolutely! That doesn't mean that God gave that person the cancer in order to reach the others; it simply means that He can take what Satan meant for evil or what the sin nature dished out in our bodies and turn it for His glory.

Someone might argue that Jesus states clearly in John 9:2 that a certain man was born blind "deliberately" so that God could show His healing power through Jesus. Let's look at the scripture together.

> *As he went along, he saw a man blind from birth.*
>
> *His disciples asked him, "Rabbi, who sinned, this man or his parents, that he was born blind?"*
>
> *"Neither this man nor his parents sinned," said Jesus, "but this happened so that the work of God might be displayed in his life.*
>
> *As long as it is day, we must do the work of him who sent me. Night is coming, when no one can work.*
>
> *While I am in the world, I am the light of the world."*

John 9:1-5

As we see in the first verse, there was a very strong belief system in those days that any illness or deformity was brought on by either your sin or the sin of your parents. Actually, many people still believe that today.

Here's what I believe Jesus was saying to the disciples concerning this man and his blindness.

First of all, note that Jesus says in verse 2, "Neither this man nor his parents sinned . . ." We know according to Romans 3:23 that all have sinned and fallen short of the glory of God, so is Jesus lying, or does He mean something else?

Second, note that as Jesus continues to talk to the disciples, the subject matter seems to change from this man's blindness to Jesus Himself.

I believe that because the disciples were focused on the sin rather than the man, Jesus was trying to change their focus from sin and judging others to God's love and forgiveness. He wasn't saying that the man and his parents had never sinned but rather that it wasn't because of individual sins that the man was born blind. By taking the focus away from sin, Jesus was saying that the man was more important than the reason he had an infirmity.

When Jesus said, "this happened," I don't believe He was just speaking about this man's blindness but rather was speaking of the effects of the sin nature itself. He could have said something like, "these things happen because sin is in the world."

And what is the "work of God" that is to be displayed in this man's life? Jesus! Light dispels darkness, and since Jesus says in verse 5 that He is the light of the world, He was talking about Himself. The darkness that He dispels is the sin nature. He could have said it like this: "These things happen because sin is in the world; however, I now have the opportunity to be displayed in this man's life as a light to expose the sin nature and expel the darkness."

How many times did Jesus tell someone after He healed them, "Your sins are forgiven."? The healing power of Jesus doesn't just heal the body but also forgives the sin.

Jesus was not saying that God caused the man to be born blind so that He could show God's mercy and grace by healing him. He was saying that the sin nature (sickness, poverty, spiritual blindness, etc.) is exposed through the works of Jesus. Jesus, being the light of the world, exposes the darkness called sin.

Whether you are a Christian or not, God loves you with an everlasting love, and He loves you regardless of your physical imperfections. Are you or your parents required to ask for a healing if you were born imperfect? No, of course not. Again, can God use you to reach millions of others through your imperfection? A resounding yes! But that just means that God can use you in spite of the handicap, not that He made you with the handicap in order to use you.

You must understand what I'm saying or you will find yourself in the ditch over this. Every truth is like a road with ditches on either side. The left ditch is non-acceptance of the truth. The right ditch is going too far with the truth and turning it into another lie (a religious doctrine). So, you either keep this in perspective and glide along in the center of the road (the truth), or you reject the truth or make a complete religion out of it and thereby trudge along in the ditch.

An example of going too far would be to say this book teaches we are all little gods who are in complete control of our own lives and therefore are not in need of God.

If you've read the Bible, then you know when God wanted to take out an entire nation, He did. When God decided He did not like how His creation turned out, He destroyed the entire world except for one family. Ultimately, God is in control. However, I hope to show you through this book how God has given us a measure of control over our own lives.

Never forget that God is:
El'Shaddai: God Almighty or God All Sufficient.
Jehovah-Rapha: our healer.
Jehovah-Tsidkenu: our righteousness.
Jehovah-Jireh: our provider.
Jehovah-Shalom: our peace.
Jehovah-Elohim: our conqueror.
Jehovah-Nissi: our banner.
Jehovah-El'Elyon: Supreme God or Most Loved God.
I AM! And that says it all.

This book is not meant to, nor will it in any way, diminish who God is but rather expose the lie that keeps us from all the promises He has already given us. God wants you to know His Word and live according to it. It's time to expose Satan's lie and stop allowing him to rob us of God's truth.

In the Dedication I mention my sister, Teresa, and the fact that she passed away. I want to share a poem my daughter wrote in response to a family member's anger toward God because of Teresa's death, as well as what life had dealt this person herself. This poem should help you see what this book is all about.

THE PEN

My life is like God's storybook
Whose pages have not been filled
He has it planned out perfectly
But opted to give free will

Instead of writing out my life
He gave me the pen to write
To make my own decisions
Of how to live my life

I made some wrong decisions
So many pains I did endure
And many times in my life
The next chapter was not sure

In the end I wrote my story
With a very bitter bite
Wondering if I should even bother
To wake up in the morning light

And when I died I asked God
Why He let me turn out this way
He pointed and said,
"You controlled the pen, so what have you to say?"

It was then and there I realized
The choices had all been mine
To write my own decisions
To make up my own mind

Many circumstances came my way
That I did not want or choose
But it was my reaction
That made me win or lose

God then showed me the book
That He had planned for my life
And I was amazed at how happy I was
Despite the same old strife

He explained that the hurt and pain
Had never been planned
But pain is simply what happens
When man is in command

God did have a plan for me
That was better than what I lived
But He kept reminding me
That I controlled the pen

Satan did not make me do it
Nor did family or friends
Every decision was my own
Because I controlled the pen.

By Tamara Green

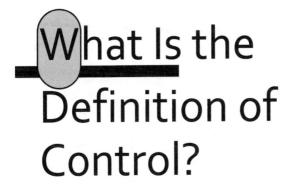What Is the Definition of Control?

I want to make sure all who read this book understand what I mean by the word control. Oftentimes a word can have several different meanings depending on the use of the word in a given sentence.

Webster defines the word control as:
to exercise restraining or directing influence over.

The Free Online Dictionary defines control as:
to exercise authoritative or dominating influence over; to direct.

Some people think of "God's control" as Him making the plans for our lives and doing all the work to bring about that plan while we just sit back and wait for it all to happen, like marionettes on a string. They believe everything is pre-destined just as it happens. How many times in the face of a disaster have you heard someone say, "There's a reason for everything." Of course, what they mean by this is: "We don't understand God's ways and can't fathom why He caused or allowed the disaster, but after all, He's in control, so we must just accept it."

I suppose one reason people believe everything that happens is orchestrated by God is due to John 15:5.

> *I am the vine; you are the branches. If a man remains in me and I in him, he will bear much fruit; apart from me you can do nothing.*

That last part of the scripture, "apart from me you can do nothing" is possibly one reason people believe the lie that "God is in control." However, we must remember that Satan takes a truth from the Word of God and twists and perverts it until it becomes a religious set of handcuffs. Many Christians are waiting around for God to do something in their lives. "I'm waiting on God to change my situation," they say. After we dig into His Word I hope to help you discover that God is waiting on you!

Think of a business that you might own and are in "control" of. You have several employees whom you've hired to help you in this business. If they use the same mentality we use with God by saying, "Well, you're in control, so we're just here to see what you can do," then you're going to be a very tired business owner.

By virtue of the definition of control, your job is to exercise restraining, directing, authoritative or dominating influence over these employees to do the work, not do the work yourself while they sit around and wait for the results. Would you pay an employee who sat around doing nothing while you do all of his work for him? I don't think so! And yet that's what we expect God to do: keep us healthy and safe, keep our kitchen cabinets and our gas tanks full, and ultimately allow us into heaven, all while we spend none or maybe just a few minutes in our lifetime fellowshipping with Him.

Why then does God tell us in John 15:5 that apart from Him we can do nothing, especially since according to Psalm 8:6 God made man ruler over all the earth?

> *You made him ruler over the works of your hands; you put everything under his feet . . .*

All throughout the Bible we're going to find that God gave us power over our lives; however, He reminds us in John 15:5 that without Him creating us in the first place we could do nothing. Without Him giving us our talents, we could do nothing. Without the knowledge He gives us, we could do nothing. This scripture, I believe, is meant to keep us humble in the midst of the awesome power He gave us over our lives. In addition, Deuteronomy 8:17-18 says—

> *You may say to yourself, "My power and the strength of my hands have produced this wealth for me."*

> *But remember the LORD your God, for it is he who gives you the ability to produce wealth, and so confirms his covenant, which he swore to your forefathers, as it is today.*

We must not forget that God created the very breath that keeps us alive, as well as the knowledge, talents, and wisdom we possess. It's what you do with those gifts that you are in control of. Like the business owner who gives the employees the resources they need to do the job, God gives us the ability and resources to do all that we do.

If God, therefore, has given us power over our own lives, who is in control?

Some people believe their "lot in life" controls their success or failure. They believe they are a product of their environment. But this too is part of Satan's lie as to who is in control.

It's not your circumstances that determine who you are or what your future will be but rather your response to those circumstances. Your response, not God's. It is your life to live and you are given the freedom to make choices each and every day. Almost every choice you make affects someone else in some way; just as other people's choices might affect you.

My very first lesson in who was in control of my life came at the age of 17. I was a very angry teenager with a chip on my shoulder the size of Texas. I blamed the world for my woes and dared anyone to say anything out of line or even look at me wrong.

When I was in the eleventh grade I took a Child Psychology class. One of our assignments was to complete a survey that asked many questions about our home life, our outlook on life, and so forth. We were then given an analysis of what this survey suggested our particular personalities were as a result of our upbringing and personal experiences in life. My analysis suggested that I was a very angry "female dog," to put it in high school terms. Of course the analysis suggested my wrongful attitude was a result of a dysfunctional family and some personal situations that I will not go into in this book.

I went to God in prayer because I didn't want to be what this survey said I was. Of course I spewed some venom about how others in my life had made me this way and how certain circumstances in my life were the cause of my misbehavior and anger.

This is when I received my first revelation knowledge of how I was in control of who I am and how my life would be. God spoke to me that day so very clearly saying, "No one can make you into who you are." I disagreed with Him and proceeded to tell Him about the things that were happening in my life (as if He didn't already know) and how it was, in fact, the cause of my anger and the chip on my shoulder. God spoke to me again and said that no one could make me into who I was. So, I made a decision that I was not going to be angry at life anymore.

My first act toward my new life was that I was going to smile. Unfortunately, my face was in the habit of looking angry so I had to practice smiling in front of a mirror. When I was at school, I plastered a smile on my face. I knew the smile looked fake, but I was determined to change the frown into a smile.

Shortly afterwards, I found myself actually feeling happier about life, regardless of the circumstances. I had a classmate tell me that he was glad to finally get to know me. He said he'd seen me in the halls many times and wanted to talk to me but because of the look on my face he was afraid I would bite his head off.

Although I thought I had completely understood what God said to me at school that day, I didn't get the full revelation until a few years later when my pastor spoke from the pulpit: "Your circumstances in life cannot make or break you. It's your response to your circumstance that causes you to fail or succeed. You can get bitter or you can get better."

Maybe it was because I was a little older or more mature at this time or maybe it was because I had begun to let go of the past hurts in my life, but this statement caused a light bulb to be turned on in my head.

I finally understood that two people could go through the same exact experience in life and turn out two entirely different ways. Why is this? If the situations were the same, and according to child psychology it's your experiences in life that make you who you are, then how can two people go through the same experience but turn out differently? It depends on their personal response to that circumstance.

One may choose to be bitter about the cards dealt them in life while the other may choose to be a better person in spite of what life dished out. No matter what your circumstance, it's up to you to become bitter or better. You are in control of the outcome.

I'm not saying people who hurt others shouldn't be held accountable for their actions. They can be prosecuted for their wrongdoing and still be forgiven by the victim and by God. If we refuse to forgive those who have wronged us, we choose to remain the victim.

Nor am I releasing parents of their responsibility to treat their children with tender loving care. Even though it's to our own benefit to respond to negative treatment with love and forgiveness, everyone needs to consider the words coming out of their mouth. I've heard parents call their children such names as "worthless," "pain in the butt," "crybaby," and such. Words have power and they can cut deeper than a knife.

People might not be so quick to speak hateful and hurtful things to others if they kept in mind that the Bible says we will have to give account for every word that comes out of our mouths. But regardless of how we've been treated by others, we can still choose to be victorious rather than remain victims.

Since there are consequences to our choices, everyone, Christian or not, will be held accountable for their choices. We could call those choices our fruits or works in life.

Going back to John 15:5, God says anyone who remains in Him will produce much fruit. Notice that the person will produce the fruit, not that God will produce the fruit in them or for them. The "fruit" in this scripture is referring to the outcome of our actions in life, or commonly referred to in the Christian realm as our works.

Here's a word picture for you that I hope will help. If you pull a branch of grapes off the vine, that branch will die and never produce again. If you just pluck the grapes but leave the branch, the branch will produce again.

So if Jesus is the vine and we are the branches, then the grapes on the branches are the fruit or works we produce in life. If we have a relationship with Jesus, then these fruits or works will be plentiful; otherwise, they'll count for nothing.

Although the Bible is clear that we cannot work our way to heaven, it is just as clear that all of our works will one day be judged by God. 1 Corinthians 3:13-15 says—

> *. . . his work will be shown for what it is, because the Day will bring it to light. It will be revealed with fire, and the fire will test the quality of each man's work.*
>
> *If what he has built survives, he will receive his reward.*
>
> *If it is burned up, he will suffer loss; he himself will be saved, but only as one escaping through the flames.*

In other words, you might make it to heaven by the skin of your teeth, thereby escaping a sentence to hell, but your fruit or works while on earth were no good. This makes it very clear to me that we are to be active in our own lives rather than our lives being predestined by God. Otherwise, God would be unfair for judging our works when they really were not our works but His.

Jesus tells us in Matthew 25:31-40 that what we do to one another is accounted to us on the day of judgment as having done it to Him. These are the types of works we will be rewarded for or condemned for. Matthew 25:31-40 reads—

> *When the Son of Man comes in his glory, and all the angels with him, he will sit on his throne in heavenly glory. All the nations will be gathered before him, and he will separate the people one from another as a shepherd separates the sheep from the goats. He will put the sheep on his right and the goats on his left.*
>
> *Then the King will say to those on his right, "Come, you who are blessed by my Father; take your inheritance, the kingdom prepared for you since the creation of the world. For I was hungry and you gave me something to eat, I was thirsty and you gave me something to drink, I was a stranger and you invited me in, I needed clothes and you clothed me, I was sick and you looked after me, I was in prison and you came to visit me."*
>
> *Then the righteous will answer him, "Lord, when did we see you hungry and feed you, or thirsty and give you something to drink? When did we see you a stranger and invite you in, or needing clothes and clothe you? When did we see you sick or in prison and go to visit you?"*

The King will reply, "I tell you the truth, whatever you did for one of the least of these brothers of mine, you did for me."

So, who is in control, God or us? Is it up to God whether we make it to heaven or not, or is it up to us? God gave clear directions on what we needed to do to enter heaven, so it's up to us to follow those directions or disregard them. I choose to be a sheep and follow His directions, not a goat who will hear, "Depart from me." I hope you make that choice too.

Unfortunately, there are many people in life who don't care or don't know that their works will be judged, so they make bad choices, choices that sometimes hurt other people. If you're someone who has been hurt by another, don't believe the lie that God knew what He was doing and allowed that for some greater purpose.

That person made a bad choice and you, unfortunately, were the recipient of that choice, but that doesn't mean you have to remain a victim.

Chapter 2

Who's in Control?

I want to use some examples from the Bible to show how God gives us control over our own lives but how He "exercises restraining, directing, authoritative and dominating influence over us." The key word here is influence, which means: A power affecting a person, thing, or course of events.

It could be written like this: God is a power that exercises influence over His creation in order to affect and direct the course of events in their lives. Why? For the purpose of bringing about all the promises of wealth, health, joy, peace, and eternal life for His beloved creation.

As I said before, the lie of Satan is that either you don't have to do anything to receive these blessings–just wait on God, or your life is just what it is so you should accept it. All of the promises of God already belong to Christians, but we must do our part to receive them, not just sit on our blessed assurances waiting for the blessings to fall from heaven as Satan would have us believe.

God says He will give you the means to get wealth, but that doesn't mean you can sit home watching soap operas all day waiting for some employer to come knocking on your door to offer you a job. If you want a job, you need to be out seeking one. You can, however, pray for God's direction on which job to take or where to even look in the first place and He will direct you. You can ask Him to open doors He wants you to go through and close doors He doesn't want you to go through, and He'll do that. However, you must be spiritually in tune with God in order to recognize His voice and be able to follow it.

The first example from the Bible I want to use is Cain, Adam and Eve's firstborn son. We read in Genesis 4:4-5, that both Cain and Abel brought offerings to God.

> *. . . The Lord looked with favor on Abel and his offer-ing, but on Cain and his offering he did not look with favor . . .*

Some believe the reason God was not pleased with Cain's offering is because it was fruits of the soil, whereas Abel's offering required the shedding of blood. I don't believe this is true.

Let's look at why God was not pleased with Cain. Going back to Genesis 4:3-4a, it reads—

> *In the course of time Cain brought some of the fruits of the soil as an offering to the Lord.*

> *But Abel brought fat portions from some of the first-born of his flock.*

The first thing we need to notice is that "in the course of time" Cain brought his offering; meaning when he got around to it. So, either it wasn't the first ripe fruits of his harvest or he had stored the firstfruits and then brought them to God at some point when he felt like it.

The second thing we notice is that the scripture says Cain brought "some of the fruits." Could it be that Cain didn't bring the best of his crops, but rather the less desirable ones? The Bible is very clear that offerings were to be perfect, without blemish. When I read the first chapter of Malachi, I often wonder if this was Cain's mistake. In Malachi 1:8 and 1:13b God is very clear how He feels about blemished sacrifices.

> ### Malachi 1:8
> *"When you bring blind animals for sacrifice, is that not wrong? When you sacrifice crippled or diseased animals, is that not wrong? Try offering them to your governor! Would he be pleased with you? Would he accept you?" says the Lord Almighty.*

> ### Malachi 1:13b
> *"When you bring injured, crippled or diseased animals and offer them as sacrifices, should I accept them from your hands?" says the Lord.*

I'm not saying this is, in fact, what Cain did. I'm just saying it's a possibility.

In contrast, Abel brought his offering from the firstborn of his flock. His offering was brought immediately from the firstfruits of his labor and was obviously not blemished.

There is no distinction between the careers these two brothers chose (Shepherd versus Farmer) but rather the heart condition of the one bringing the offering to the Lord. Cain obviously did not have God first in his life. He did not excitedly obey by bringing his firstfruits to God, but rather eventually got around to it; or he didn't bring his best fruits but rather some less desirable ones.

Maybe he was somewhat like those people who go to church on Easter and Christmas but don't have time the rest of the year, or they only obey when they don't have anything else to occupy their time. They're not giving their best but rather a token sacrifice hoping it will please God and thereby pleasing their own religious spirit.

So here's where Cain was in control but blew it. God says to Cain in Genesis 4:6—

> *Then the Lord said to Cain, "Why are you angry? Why is your face downcast? If you do what is right, will you not be accepted? But if you do not do what is right, sin is crouching at your door; it desires to have you, but you must master it."*

This scripture confirms that Cain did something wrong when bringing the sacrifice to God. Can you see that God was telling Cain he was in control of the blessings or curses he would receive? God tells him that if he does what is right then he will be blessed, but if he does not do what is right then sin, or evil, is near to destroy him. Also note, God didn't say He would destroy Cain but that sin wanted to destroy him. God further tells Cain that he must master this sin. Cain, not God, had to take an active role in mastering the sin in his life.

Cain was probably already plotting his brother's death in his heart. Knowing this, God was trying to warn Cain to master the sin of murder that he was harboring. Again, notice that God did not say, "Let me remove that sin of murder from your heart, Cain." God told Cain he must master the sin. Cain controlled whether the sin was in his heart or not. God didn't put it there. Satan didn't put it there. Cain put it there because of his own jealousy.

Did you know that Satan can't do anything to you without your permission? Remember the song, "Que Sera, Sera"? The lyrics are: "Whatever will be, will be, the future's not ours to see." That's hogwash and part of this whole lie of Satan's! Satan wants us to accept this concept of whatever will be will be so we won't accept the truth that we can affect what happens in our lives. I'm not talking about fortune-telling here, I'm talking about obeying God's Word and taking authority over Satan's plans and stopping them.

We read all throughout the Bible this theme: God says IF you do, THEN I'll do. From the beginning of time God has given us control over our own lives with the promise of IF we do what He says, then He'll do what He promises. The Bible is full of IFs and THENs; our part and then God's response.

Deuteronomy 28 tells us our blessings come through obedience, and curses come through disobedience. I would strongly encourage you to put this book down for a moment and read Deuteronomy 28.

Who makes the choice to obey or disobey? Every one of us, every day of our lives! As parents, think of how we raise our children. We, too, use the IF and THEN principle. If the child is obedient then blessings are given in the form of material items or privileges. If the child is disobedient then punishment or removal of privileges is the result. Isn't that what Deuteronomy 28 says? Let's look at some of the verses.

Verse 1 says IF you obey THEN God will promote you—

> *If you fully obey the LORD your God and carefully follow all his commands I give you today, THEN the LORD your God will set you high above all the nations on earth.*

I may not be in a position of power over the earth, but when God told me where He wanted me to work and I obeyed him, I received two raises and a promotion to supervisor within four months.

Verse 9 says IF you keep God's command and walk in His ways, THEN God will call you His child, His holy people—

> *The LORD will establish you as his holy people, as he promised you on oath, if you keep the commands of the LORD your God and walk in his ways.*

People at work know I'm a Christian without me ever saying a word about God. I had a young woman approach me one day for some counseling. She told me she didn't know why she was coming to me, she just felt like she could trust me and that I would give her good advice. I had the wonderful opportunity to explain that the horrible things that happened to her as a child were not God's plan but rather the acts of someone with a sinful nature. I was able to help her work on forgiving those people so that she could become victorious rather than focusing on having been the victim.

When you truly walk in the ways of God, people will recognize you as God's child. I had a customer approach me once and say that he appreciated my smile and kindness and knew I was a Christian. When I asked him how he knew I was a Christian since we had never spoken before, he said that I had a glow about me. That glow is a physical mark of being a child of the Most High God.

When you belong to God, through the personal decision of accepting Jesus Christ as your Lord and Savior, and you walk in the love of God, people will know it without being told.

Verse 13 says IF you pay attention when the Lord speaks to you and follow His directions and commands, THEN you will always be on top and never on the bottom, the head and not the tail—

The LORD will make you the head, not the tail. If you pay attention to the commands of the LORD your God that I give you this day and carefully follow them, you will always be at the top, never at the bottom.

Ultimately, we decide whether or not we receive the blessings God has already given us. If we fully obey the Lord, pay attention, and carefully follow His commands, then we will be blessed.

Another example I'd like to use from the Bible is the story of Jonah and the Ninevites. It's a very interesting story, but in a nutshell God tells Jonah, one of his prophets, to go to a city called Nineveh and preach against their wickedness because He, God, is going to overturn the city. Jonah does not want to preach to the Ninevites because he doesn't want them saved, so he runs from God. In the end, however, God gets His way. Jonah obeys God, and the Ninevites repent and turn from their wicked ways. But Jonah had to make the choice to obey. He could have drug his feet, so to speak, for years. He was in control of his decisions although God influenced his decision by controlling the circumstances around him.

Remember that control means to exercise restraining or directing influence over; and influence means the power affecting a person, thing, or course of events. God brought about situations in Jonah's life to make him realize that he was not doing what God wanted him to do. Jonah then had to make the final decision to yield or not to yield to God.

So where does God's control end and our control begin?

God says in Ezekiel 3:18-19—

> *When I say to a wicked man, 'You will surely die,' and you do not warn him or speak out to dissuade him from his evil ways in order to save his life, that wicked man will die for his sin, and I will hold you accountable for his blood.*
>
> *But if you do warn the wicked man and he does not turn from his wickedness or from his evil ways, he will die for his sin; but you will have saved yourself.*

God knows the end before the beginning. He knows the heart of every human being ever born. He knows exactly what it will take to direct them to where He wants them, and where He wants them is ultimately in heaven with Him.

He also knows exactly who is going to reject Him, but He still tries to influence that person. I believe not one person will be able to stand before God on the day of judgment and say that He did not give them all the chances they needed.

Had Jonah refused to preach to the Ninevites, two things could have happened. 1) The Ninevites would have perished at the hand of God and been lost for all eternity because of their sins; or 2) God would have found someone else to preach to them. In either scenario Jonah would be held accountable for any Ninevite who perished without repenting.

God's control begins with influencing people to do His will, whether that will concerns themselves or someone else. My control begins with the obedience or the disobedience of that influence.

God wants all of His creation to enter heaven upon their death. He does not wish for anyone, no matter how wicked they were, to perish and suffer eternity in hell. But He uses people, you and I, to reach the lost. Either we obey or we don't. And there's a consequence to every decision we make in life.

Let's look at a more positive situation in which our obedience or disobedience affects others.

I remember a story a pastor told once about a missionary who was ministering to a remote tribal people in a third world country. God told him to teach on tithes and offerings. Since the missionary felt these people didn't have anything to give, especially money since they didn't use the monetary system that we Americans use, he promptly informed God that he would not teach these people about giving.

When most Americans think of "giving," they immediately think of money. God, however, wants to bless His children in every area of their lives, not just financially.

So, God informed the missionary that because of his disobedience he would be held accountable for the tribe's lack. Suddenly the missionary saw this from a different perspective—personal accountability—so he agrees to teach the lesson.

After having explained the principle of seedtime and harvest, tithes and offerings, the missionary explained that at the next service they would take up an offering. The people were obedient and brought what little they had, such as a chicken egg, a pint of milk, and maybe a few cobs of corn or a little wheat. Immediately God blessed their animals and crops, and they began to live in abundance.

Soon they were taking up baskets of eggs, gallons of milk, and an abundance of crops at every service. The other tribes in the surrounding area began to notice the increase and came to inquire as to what this tribe was doing different. Their response? "Let me tell you about our God!"

The missionary could have chosen not to "burden" the people with the message of tithes and offerings and they could have continued on as they were and would not have had the opportunity to bring the other tribes to the saving knowledge of Jesus Christ. Do you see how the missionary was in control?

God gave instruction, the missionary at first chose not to obey, but then by the authoritative influence of God, the missionary changed his mind and chose to obey. All God said was, "Okay, you can choose not to obey me, but you will be held accountable for their lack." In other words, the tribe would never have known life could be any different, and the missionary would be held accountable on the day of judgment for all the lives of the other tribes who may never have come to know God, as well as the lack of provisions in his group.

The tribal people were in control of their blessings as well because they could have chosen not to give and thereby stop the blessings God had planned for them. Please don't just see the materialistic blessing in this story. This tribe will now be credited with the possible hundreds or thousands of souls saved from eternity in hell because of their obedience. That's worth more than all the money on this planet.

God was not just interested in improving this tribe's lifestyle, He was interested in this tribe being blessed so they could be a blessing to others. God's ultimate goal in all that He does is to reach the lost and thereby enlarge the Kingdom of God. Two scriptures come to mind here.

Matthew 6:33
But seek first his kingdom and his righteousness and all these things will be given to you as well.

Matthew 7:11
If you, then, though you are evil, know how to give good gifts to your children, how much more will your Father in heaven give good gifts to those who ask him!

God blesses us so we can be a blessing to others! One thing we must remember when we're asking for a financial blessing from God is that He's not going to drop a hundred dollar bill out of the sky and into your hands. He's going to use some-one who is willing to obey Him to meet your needs. Also, if you've stopped seeking the blessor and are only seeking the blessings, you are out of fellowship with God and will not see the blessings.

That's why the scripture above says, "seek first His kingdom." There's nothing wrong with teaching on God's blessings, but it must be taught the correct way.

Included in "all these things" in the above scripture are such things as health in your body, wisdom in your job, safety from the enemy, as well as meeting your financial needs. The problem some pastors and congregations fall into is they focus on the money aspect of God's blessings and stop focus-ing on Him.

I would like to share a couple of personal stories with you now; stories that helped to give me this revelation knowledge concerning the control I have over my own life.

Back in 1994 I was stationed at the Air Force Academy in Colorado Springs, Colorado. I spent many of my lunch hours running to keep in shape (since the military seemed to think this was important). One day I chose to run a mountain trail that intersected with the road I normally ran on. Shortly after starting out I sensed "danger, turn around." My first thought was that the enemy was trying to scare me. My pastor had been teaching recently on the power of our words so, relying on the Word of God, I rebuked this thought quoting that God does not give me a spirit of fear. A little while later I again sensed "danger, turn around." Irritated with Satan for bothering me again, I ordered him to "get thee behind me," followed by "no weapon formed against me can prosper." My mind was thinking of such dangers as bears, mountain lions, or snakes. What happened next I can only explain as a spiritual experience.

I heard a voice say, "If you cross this line you will force my hand and I will not be able to protect you." I cannot tell you now whether this was an audible voice or just a voice in my spirit but I can tell you it got my attention. Knowing that Satan was not in the business of protecting me, my lightning fast mind (as Pastor Mark used to say) concluded that this wasn't Satan after all but rather my Heavenly Father. With my foot literally in mid-air I could see a line drawn in the dirt across the trail (in the spirit). I had a choice to bring my foot down and cross that line anyway and take my chances or obey God and turn around.

I chose to turn around and get the heck off the trail as fast as I could. As I was hiking back down, God gave me a vision of five young men coming up the trail toward me. Two of them dropped off the trail as if looking for something on the side of the mountain while the other three continued on the trail toward me. As the three passed me, the other two came back onto the trail in front of me. I now had two in front of me and three behind me. Suddenly, the men behind me attacked and the two in front joined in. I'll leave the result of the attack to your imagination. Remember, this was a vision that ran through my mind on my way back down the trail; however, I was not yet aware that it was a vision from God. I really thought I was just letting my imagination get away with me.

The road I normally ran on was in the shape of a horseshoe with this trail leading off from the center of the curved part. I would access the road from the west, run to the east end, turn around and run back to the west end. As I came off the trail onto the road, I chose to pick up at that location and just run my normal route. I reached the east end of the road, turned around and headed back to the west end. As I approached the curve in the road where the trail-head intersected, I noticed a white car parked there with five young men outside of the car. Three of them were on the trail and two of them were on the side of the trail looking on the ground for something, or so it was supposed to appear. I noticed, however, these two men would occasionally look back down the road at me. At this point I realized that God had given me a vision of what the "danger" had been. I started praying, but I also picked up a big stick, crossed to the other side of the road, and continued to jog with as much confidence as I could display.

I had been taught that a predator, even a human predator, is fueled by the display of fear from its victim and therefore young women should walk with confidence because this tends to discourage the predator from attacking. By the time I passed the trail-head, all five men were well on their way up the mountain.

I asked God why He didn't just show me the vision in the first place when I first decided to take this trail rather than letting me continue until the third warning. He said it was because I needed to learn to hear and recognize His voice. God explained to me that if I had been on the trail when I met up with these men, then what He showed me in the vision would have certainly come to pass. I would have been left on the mountain dead. Because I was on the open road when I encountered them, the risk was too great so they chose not to attack.

Yes, I said they CHOSE not to attack. Every act of evil is an act of choice just as every act of obedience is an act of choice. Satan cannot make anyone do anything. Even with my display of confidence and regardless of the open road and broad daylight, they could have chosen to attack.

I learned through this experience that even though I have control over situations in my life, I serve an awesome God who watches my every move and the move of others around me in order to protect me WHEN I listen and obey. I hope you can see through this story how God is in control in that He knew exactly what was going to happen to me that day, yet how I was in control in that I could have disobeyed God which would have, as He said, "forced His hand" of protection from me.

Someone might ask, "Why did God take chances with your life like that?" I don't look at it like that. God knew every choice I would make and every choice those young men would make. There are an infinite number of variables that could have occurred with this story. For example, let's say I continued to interpret the sense of danger as coming from Satan just to scare me and therefore continued to hike. Because I belong to God, He could have caused some sort of obstruction to keep those men from getting to the trail while I was there.

Have you ever noticed that God does things in multiple layers? What do I mean by that? Anytime God does something, there seems to be multiple purposes behind it. Whenever He says something, there seems to be multiple interpretations, all of them being correct. My favorite example of this is found in John 18:4-6—

> *Jesus, knowing all that was going to happen to him, went out and asked them, "Who is it you want?"*
>
> *"Jesus of Nazareth," they replied.*
>
> *"I am he," Jesus said. . . . When Jesus said "I am he," they drew back and fell to the ground.*

If Jesus already knew what was going to happen to Him, why did He ask the soldiers who they were looking for, and why did they fall to the ground at Jesus' answer?

When Moses asked God who He was supposed to say sent him, God responded with "I am." When Jesus said the words "I am," He was making a declaration that He was God. The words "I am" were so powerful they knocked the soldiers to the ground. In one layer, so to speak, Jesus was simply telling the soldiers He was who they were looking for;

yet in another layer, Jesus was making a very important declaration to the world. That is just so awesome to me!

Another example is when Jesus died on the cross. It "just so happened" that Jesus was crucified on the same day as two thieves. I believe the two thieves represent all of mankind; we're all guilty of sin and deserve punishment. The two thieves also represent "free-will choice." We all have the right to choose life eternal with God or everlasting damnation in hell separated from God.

One thief mocked Jesus and chose not to believe He was the Son of God, therefore "choosing" eternal separation from Him. The other thief chose to believe, and Jesus' response to him was that he would be with Jesus in paradise. This is the choice that we all have to make; some will go the way of the thief who did not believe, and some will go the way of the thief who did believe.

Jesus being crucified between the two choices shows that He stands in the gap between heaven and hell. God was teaching us multiple lessons on that day. One, Jesus is the ultimate sacrifice for our sins; He paid the price for us. Two, we must all make the choice for ourselves whether we accept Jesus Christ as our Lord and Savior and whether we spend eternity in heaven or hell. And three, that the throne room is now accessible by each and every one of us, not just the priests. How was this demonstrated?

As soon as Jesus died, the curtain in the temple that separated the Holy Place from the Most Holy Place was torn in two from top to bottom signifying that all believers could now come into the presence of God Almighty. God is so awesome!!!

For anyone not familiar with the temple rules, you can read in the Bible, Leviticus 16, where God tells Moses to make sure Aaron, the first temple priest, knows he's not to come into the Most Holy Place whenever he chooses. He, and all priests to succeed him, were to enter the Most Holy Place only once a year and must go through a rather specific ritual before and after entering. Then after Jesus' death on the cross we're told in Hebrews 10:19-22—

> *Therefore, brothers, since we have confidence to enter the Most Holy Place by the blood of Jesus,*
>
> *by a new and living way opened for us through the curtain, that is, his body,*
>
> *and since we have a great priest over the house of God,*
>
> *let us draw near to God with a sincere heart in full assurance of faith, having our hearts sprinkled to cleanse us from a guilty conscience and having our bodies washed with pure water.*

So now Christians are allowed to come boldly before the throne of God without ritualistic cleansing or a blood sacrifice. Jesus' blood did all of that for us the day He chose to die on the cross for us. How can anyone not want to serve such an awesome God.

Getting back to the hiking story. Knowing the choices that were going to be made, I believe God chose to use this as a teaching moment for me. I can't express enough how much this experience has helped me to understand God and how close it has brought us. God did not take chances with my life; He improved it through this experience. I've often wondered if these guys were delayed by having car trouble or ran into some sort of traffic congestion just long enough for me to get back down the trail but still within sight of it. That would be just like my God!

God has a plan for our lives and that plan is nothing but good. Look again at what Jeremiah 29:11-14 says—

> *"For I know the plans I have for you," declares the LORD, "plans to prosper you and not to harm you, plans to give you hope and a future.*
>
> *Then you will call upon me and come and pray to me, and I will listen to you.*
>
> *You will seek me and find me when you seek me with all your heart.*
>
> *I will be found by you," declares the LORD . . .*

Unfortunately, there are evil people out there and an enemy who hates God and hates His people. We all have a will of our own. We are not puppets, with God as the master puppeteer. I hope you're beginning to see this truth now. People who are evil do not listen to the voice of God and therefore they do whatever pleases them. But God gives us wisdom, He gives us the Holy Spirit to speak to us, and He sends His guardian angels to cause things to happen for our benefit and protection. Psalm 103:2-5 says—

> *Praise the LORD, O my soul, and forget not all his benefits—*
>
> *who forgives all your sins and heals all your diseases,*
>
> *who redeems your life from the pit and crowns you with love and compassion,*
>
> *who satisfies your desires with good things so that your youth is renewed like the eagle's.*

Now let's fast forward to the year 2006 and in the state of Michigan for yet another lesson from my merciful God on how I'm in control of my life and how He influences everything about me when I let Him. I'm now the supervisor of the night shift freight team at a well-known retail chain. God spoke to me one day while in prayer that I needed to start speaking these words out loud while driving to work: "No animal will cross my path, there will be no accidents or injuries." Since I had been taught by my spiritual father on the importance and the power of our words, I obeyed God and spoke this every day for weeks.

One night as I was running late for work I rushed out the door distracted and frustrated. As I was driving to work, I was thinking about the events of the day and what I needed to accomplish at work and neglected to speak the words God had instructed. I noticed up ahead and to my left a herd of deer preparing to cross the road. Since they were still on the other side of a ditch, I didn't think they would cross just yet but I let off the accelerator anyway. As my attention was on the deer, I noticed in my peripheral vision something in the road further ahead. I turned my focus back to the road and noticed a raccoon was crossing. I remember thinking, "It's almost to the center of the road so there's no real danger of me hitting it, but I'll just move over to the right a little bit to make sure my driver's side tire doesn't hit it." All of a sudden I noticed that my vehicle was sliding sideways toward an eight-foot deep ditch on my left. I immediately went from the confusion of "what is going on here" to speaking out loud, "God help me! I'm out of control." I remember saying several times, "God help me," and "Jesus, You've got to help me." I didn't mean this in a demanding way but rather in a way expressing there's nothing I can do, only Jesus can help me now.

I was driving between 55 and 60 when I first saw the deer and let off the accelerator. We all know how quickly a vehicle slows down when the accelerator is released. It was several seconds from the time I took my foot off the gas pedal to when I saw the raccoon. I still remember my foot being poised over the brake when I first saw the raccoon. I then steered the vehicle to the right, and although at this point I'm sure I at least put my foot back onto the gas pedal to prepare to accelerate, I don't specifically recall accelerating. In any event, it's at this point that the vehicle began sliding out of control.

Suddenly the tires hit the shoulder of the road on my left which sent the vehicle airborne, crashing down into the middle of the road on its nose, and then rolling three times. The vehicle finally came to a stop right side up. The motor was racing louder and louder and smoke was pouring from the hood. I thought the engine was going to catch on fire so I tried to open my door to flee. The door wouldn't open; however, the window was shattered so I crawled out. Although I was shook up from the rollercoaster ride, I didn't think I had any major injuries so I declined the ambulance ride to the emergency room.

The police officer at the scene kept saying, "I can't believe you walked away from that." It was too dark for me to see the vehicle so I didn't completely grasp why he said that. I did end up going to the emergency room the following morning with a slight head injury and a muscle injury to my neck and right shoulder from the seatbelt, but nothing major. As a matter of fact, when my family doctor saw the pictures of the vehicle, he asked me why I walked away from a major accident with only minor injuries when he's had patients who've died from major injuries sustained in minor accidents. I had the privilege of spending the next hour or so talking about God's protection over His children and the power of our words.

Here is the totaled Durango.

The accident occurred on a Monday night around 9 p.m. Due to the slight concussion which caused the room to spin from time to time, the doctor put me on bed rest so I had not seen the vehicle since the night of the accident. On Thursday I decided I wanted to get out of bed and see it. My stomach tied up in knots as I stood there examining the damage. The vehicle looked like some metal crushing monster had attacked and crunched all but the area around the driver's seat. It looked like there had been a powerful bubble around me. Even though the glass was broken out and the door was jammed so I couldn't open it, you can still see there is minimal damage around the driver's seat (see photo on page 44).

I knew my God had been at work that night, even though I failed Him by being too preoccupied to remember to speak the protection He told me to speak. I believe God was trying to save me from that accident altogether by instructing

me to speak the words He told me to speak. Even in my act of negligence, however, I believe because I called out to Him (the power of words) in the midst of the trouble, He was able to save me. Proverbs 18:21 tells us—

The tongue has the power of life and death, and those who love it will eat its fruit.

I remember thinking immediately after the accident that I was not going to give Satan any glory for this; that I must have done something wrong to cause the vehicle to lose control. I actually convinced myself that I had swerved to miss the raccoon which somehow put the vehicle into a slide. But God kept bringing back to my memory that I had not swerved but rather moved slightly to the right. Losing control just didn't make any sense to me if that were the case. As God showed me again a vision of the accident, I saw the deer, then the raccoon, then me turning the wheel slightly to the right, and then a blank, like the picture screen blanks out for a second, and then I see myself sliding sideways. I still do not know exactly what caused me to lose control or why God doesn't let me see this blank section in the vision. I believe the enemy was directly and physically responsible for this accident. Possibly what took place during the "blank" section is supernatural and therefore not visible to me.

The insurance company called and wanted to know the mileage on the vehicle so my husband was checking that out on Thursday while I was standing there giving God praise for the miracle. He looked over at me and said, "You have to come see this." The odometer read 66619.

Now, you can dismiss this as just a coincidence, but I knew that I knew at that moment that either Satan was making sure I knew he was attempting to kill me or God was letting me know that Satan was responsible. The more I thought about it the more I believe it was God speaking to me and letting me know that the enemy was at work against me.

God knows every plan Satan has against every human on this earth, and He knew Satan had planned an auto accident for me. That's why He told me to speak the words He gave me several weeks before concerning animals crossing my path. God doesn't want His children to suffer at the hands of Satan so we must listen to Him when He forewarns us of impending danger.

I may have lost a vehicle and suffered a physical discomfort for a few months, but what is that compared to my life? I learned once again that it was I who gave Satan the opportunity to take me out by neglecting to speak safety over myself as God had warned me I needed to do. I can't blame Satan because I gave him the open door, and I can't blame God because He forewarned me. I had control.

When you hear a still small voice inside of you say not to go a certain route or you sense danger or that something's just not quite right, that is God exercising His authoritative and dominating influence over you to help you.

So many people tell God they don't want Him interfering in their lives, but then when something bad happens, they immediately want to know why a loving God would allow such things. If you want God's protection and His blessings, then God must be a life-style, not a life-raft.

od's Divine Influence

The Bible shows us in different stories how God takes what Satan meant for evil and turns it for His good. There are times, however, when God actually uses Satan to bring about His divine plan for our lives. One such story is about a young man named Joseph.

Joseph was one of twelve sons born to a man named Jacob. Joseph was Jacob's favorite son. Most of us are familiar with the story of Joseph and his coat of many colors.

Naturally, Joseph's brothers were jealous of him for being dad's favorite. After Joseph had a couple of dreams that insinuate his brothers and parents would one day bow down to him, his brothers became even more jealous. It's bad enough he's their father's favorite, but now Joseph thinks he's going to rule over them! Not if they can help it!

In Genesis 37:19 the brothers plot to kill Joseph. The oldest brother, Reuben, convinces them not to kill him themselves but rather throw him into a cistern in the middle of the desert and let him die there. Reuben intended to rescue little brother later and send him home to daddy. However, while the brothers are resting and eating, a caravan of Ishmaelites happen to pass by on their way to Egypt. One of the brothers sees an opportunity to be rid of little brother without shedding blood. So, 17 year-old Joseph is sold to the Ishmaelites who in turn sell him to the Egyptians as a slave. Joseph's story is found in Genesis, chapters 39-41, and is a great example of how Christians should act. Regardless of his situation, Joseph did everything with excellence and, as far as we can tell, without complaint.

In a nutshell, the story goes like this: Joseph is falsely accused and put into prison. God gives Pharaoh a dream of an approaching famine, but he doesn't understand this so he asks for someone to interpret this dream for him. Joseph is brought out of prison to interpret the dream. Not only does Joseph interpret the dream, but he also advises Pharaoh of a solution to ensure his people survive the famine. Pharaoh is so impressed with this wisdom that he puts Joseph in charge of the whole land of Egypt. Talk about a promotion! From the prison to the palace!! I wonder if Joseph thought that his visions from God were finally coming true, even though he didn't know if he'd ever see his family again.

The famine hits as prophesied and affects the whole world (Gen. 41:57). Jacob learns there is food in Egypt so he sends ten of his sons there to buy grain. You can read the interesting account of Joseph's reaction to his brothers' presence in Genesis 42-47. Finally, he tells his brothers not to be afraid, that he's not going to punish them for what they did to him because it was God's intention for him to be in the position he is in now in order to save his family. What Satan meant for evil—jealousy and hatred—God used to bring about His plan—saving the Israelites.

It was 13 years between the time Joseph was sold as a slave and the fulfillment of the dream God gave him, that of being a ruler. Sometimes we think because nothing seems to be happening right now, God must have forgotten us. Or maybe when things are going all wrong, we think we must have missed it or done something wrong to change God's mind.

There were many factors that had to take place in order to get Joseph into this position of ruler. I wonder if the caravan of Ishmaelites changed course for some odd reason which brought them by Jacob's sons sitting in the middle of the desert. What would have happened if the caravan decided to stay on the course they were on or if Joseph's brothers had chosen another location to stop and eat? What if Reuben had chosen to take sides with his younger brothers and helped to kill Joseph? There are many variables along the way that could have been changed by man's will; however, I believe God would have found another way to bring about His plan and purpose.

The Bible says many people died during that famine. I wonder if the Israelite clan would have all died during those seven years of famine had it not been for Joseph. Do you know why Jesus is called the Lion of the Tribe of Judah? Who is Judah? He is Joseph's brother who talked the others into selling Joseph rather than killing him. God had already planned the lineage of Jesus through Judah and the survival of Judah through Joseph.

Had Joseph not been alive to become ruler over Egypt, Jacob and his sons might have died in the famine and then we couldn't call Jesus the Lion of the Tribe of Judah. Do you think there could have been some divine influence over Judah's decision, whether he was aware of it or not?

Another story in the Bible of how God used Satan to fulfill His purpose is the story of Job. We're told at the beginning of the book that Job was a "blameless and upright man." But we're also told in verse 5 that Job had a fear that his children would curse God during one of their many parties, so it was his custom to act as priest over them and have them purified as well as offer burnt sacrifices for each of them after their parties.

The chapter goes on to tell us how the angels came to present themselves before the Lord; and Satan, the accuser of the brethren, came with them. God asked Satan if he had considered Job. I believe what God was saying here is that Satan had nothing in which to accuse Job since he was "blameless and upright, a man who fears God and shuns evil." Of course, Satan replies that Job fears God for selfish reasons, being that God has blessed everything in Job's life. I believe this is the key of why God even started this dialog with Satan.

This is just my opinion, but I believe God knew that Job was dealing with a bit of pride that would one day cost him his relationship with God. I believe Job's fear that his children would sin during one of their parties was focused more on what that would do to his reputation than on his children's salvation. Let me explain why I believe this and then I'll explain what I believe God's plan was for Job.

After Job loses all of his financial success and all of his children, we read in Chapter 1, verse 22—

> In all this, Job did not sin by charging God with wrongdoing.

Then we read in chapter 3, verse 25, how after Job is afflicted with boils over his entire body, he admits to his selfish fears.

"What I feared has come upon me; what I dreaded has happened to me.

I have no peace, no quietness; I have no rest, but only turmoil."

It would take another book to discuss the dialog between Job and his three friends, but what I noticed was Job's attitude of "woe is me." His friends were upset about this also since Job had obviously instructed others that you must take the good with the bad, and yet here he was in all his piety complaining about having done nothing wrong and yet suffering as though he had.

Then we read in chapter 38 God's response to Job who said in chapter 31:35, "Let the Almighty answer me." So God does, starting in verse 2—

"Who is this that darkens my counsel with words with out knowledge? Brace yourself like a man; I will question you, and you shall answer me.

Where were you when I laid the earth's foundation? Tell me, if you understand. Who marked off its dimensions? Surely you know!"

This is why I believe Job was dealing with an issue of pride. Why would God ask a mere man such questions? It sounds like God is being sarcastic with Job—"Surely you know!" I think Job was starting to get a "big head" because of his position in society. He apparently was considered one of the wisest and most righteous men around.

Pride is what caused Lucifer to fall from heaven. Pride will cause us to fall every time.

God was not willing to lose Job over this issue of pride so He had to bring him down a peg or two in order to remove the pride. This is where God used Satan to fulfill His purpose. Had Satan known that eventually pride would cost Job his salvation, he would have never taken the bait from God to attack Job; he would have just left him to his own destruction.

The perfect story of how God used Satan to bring about His plan and purpose is the story of Jesus. God's plan, which ultimately included Jesus' death on the cross, was for our benefit. God Himself was willing to take the penalty for our sinful choices in life which would result in our death and separation from Him. Isn't it interesting that the Sadducees and Pharisees thought they were doing something great by influencing people to kill Jesus, when it was God's plan all along? I bet Satan was dancing a jig thinking he had influenced people to persecute Jesus. However, we're told in Colossians 1:19-23 concerning Jesus—

> *For God was pleased to have all his fullness dwell in him, and through him to reconcile to himself all things, whether things on earth or things in heaven, by making peace through his blood, shed on the cross.*
>
> *Once you were alienated from God and were enemies in your minds because of your evil behavior. But now he has reconciled you by Christ's physical body through death to present you holy in his sight, without blemish and free from accusation—if you continue in your faith, established and firm, not moved from the hope held out in the gospel.*

There's that IF and THEN again. If you walk in faith, then the hope given through the death and resurrection of Jesus Christ is yours. Praise God!!

We could say that it was man's idea to beat Jesus, but that too was God's plan all along as we see in the Book of Isaiah, which was written sometime between 681 to 701 years before Christ's birth. Isaiah writes in 53:4-5—

Surely he took up our infirmities and carried our sorrows, yet we considered him stricken by God, smitten by him, and afflicted.

But he was pierced for our transgressions, he was crushed for our iniquities, the punishment that brought us peace was upon him, and by his wounds we are healed.

This was prophesied 700 years before Jesus was born!! As we see in 1 Peter 2:24, the prophesy came true—

He himself bore our sins in his body on the tree, so that we might die to sins and live for righteousness; by his wounds you have been healed.

Jesus endured stripes on His back so that we may be healed of sicknesses. That was God's plan from the beginning of time, knowing that His creation would sin and therefore bring sickness and disease upon themselves.

So, what am I saying about these stories as far as who is in control? Joseph was told by God that he would one day be a ruler. He may not have known why or when he was going to become a ruler, but he had the word of God to stand on that he would. When things began to unravel in his life at the young age of 17, he could have easily become bitter and rejected God's word (the dreams). When he was falsely accused and sent to jail, he could have become bitter and rejected God. But all through Joseph's uncomfortable situations he chose to become better because he knew what God had told him.

I believe God gave Joseph the dreams concerning his future so that he had something to hold on to during the storms of life which, of course, God knew were going to happen. God chose Joseph to be the savior of his people, but Joseph had a free will and could have denied his brothers any food and could have let them starve.

Job chose to live a blameless and upright life; however, a spirit of pride was creeping in. God could have simply given Satan permission to take Job's life rather than afflicting him in any other way, which would have secured Job's salvation. Apparently Job's job on earth wasn't done though, so God had to get his attention and get his focus back on track. Job, however, could have cursed God at any point of his ordeal and lost his salvation. Apparently his love and fear for God was stronger than the pride. Of course, God knew this!

Jesus also had a free will and was in control of His own life. He could have chosen not to suffer the beatings and not to die on the cross. Jesus Himself tells us in Matthew 26:53—

> *Do you think I cannot call on my Father, and he will at once put at my disposal more than twelve legions of angels? But how then would the Scriptures be fulfilled that say it must happen in this way?*

Jesus, having control over His own life as a free-will agent, also had control as the third part of the Godhead. The Bible says in John 1:1 that Jesus and God are one.

> *In the beginning was the Word, and the Word was with God, and the Word was God. He was with God in the beginning.*

We read in 1 John 4:8 that God is love, not that He has love or created love, but rather IS love. Matthew 5:17 tells us that

Jesus came to fulfill the law. Romans 13:10 says love is the fulfillment of the law.

This bears repeating! God IS love. Jesus and God are one. Therefore, Jesus IS love. Love is the fulfillment of the law. Why is this important? Because Jesus could have at any point in the painful treatment He received from man said, "No, I don't want to do this." He could have made the choice after His first beating to stop everything. He could have decided after they pierced His head with thorns and ripped out His beard— not shaved it, ripped it out with their bare hands— that it was too physically painful to continue. He could have called 12 legions of angels to smite the people who were doing this to Him.

He CHOSE to love instead. He loved us enough to go through one of the cruelest methods of punishment and death for sins He did not commit. As the song says, "He paid the price He did not owe because we owed a price we could not pay." What an awesome God we serve!

Let me stray from the subject matter of this chapter a moment. Christians are supposed to walk in that same love. If we would grab ahold of the principle of walking in love, we could make such a difference in the world today!

I've always marveled at one of the early Christians named Stephen in the Book of Acts. He obviously learned the art of walking in love. After having just been the victim of false testimony, he looked up to heaven and saw Jesus standing at the right hand of God the Father. While he was being stoned with boulders— not little rocks that fit in the palm of your hand— for something he had not done, he looked up to heaven and asked God not to hold this sin against those people. That's love!

Put yourself in Stephen's place and ask yourself if you would do the same. You're sitting in a courtroom having been accused of a crime you did not commit. The prosecutor has put several people on the stand who've lied about you, and it's becoming pretty clear you're going to be convicted and sentenced to death. Would you bow your head in prayer and ask God not to hold this sin against these people? First Peter 4:8 says—

> *. . . love covers over a multitude of sins.*

I believe God would have saved Stephen had he cried out for Him to. It's just my opinion, but I believe that when Stephen looked up and saw Jesus, he made the choice in his heart to go home. The Bible says in Acts 7:59—

> *While they were stoning him, Stephen prayed, "Lord Jesus, receive my spirit." Then he fell on his knees and cried out, "Lord, do not hold this sin against them."When he had said this, he fell asleep.*

Now, back to God's divine influence. The stoning of Stephen was the beginning of an influential time in another man's life, Saul of Tarsus. You can read the story of Saul in Acts 9:1-31. Saul truly believed he was doing the right thing by having Christians arrested, jailed, and sometimes killed.

Not all acts done in the name of religion are done with God's approval. It was certainly not God's plan for the early Christians to be murdered by religious hard-hearted men.

Starting with Saul watching the stoning of Stephen, we follow Saul's very ambitious attempt to rid the country of a group of people he believed to be blaspheming his God. It wasn't until Jesus spoke to him on the road to Damascus that

Saul realized Jesus Christ was, in fact, the true Son of God. This was a remarkable act of divine influence.

How many of us Christians would love to have a Damascus experience where Jesus speaks to us audibly about what we're doing or what He wants us to do? And yet, how many of us are as diligent at serving God as Saul thought he was?

We read in the Bible how Saul (now renamed Paul) shows the same ambitious enthusiasm for Jesus Christ as he showed against Him. God used divine influence to change the course of Paul's life who then changed the course of the early Christian church.

As Christians, we sometimes look at our own gifts and talents and think we know where and how God can best use us, or rather how we can best help God. God chose to use Paul, a Jew very well versed in the Jewish laws and customs, to witness to the Gentiles whom the Jews considered dogs of society.

Sometimes we tell God that we're available to do something He asks only when it fits our own perceived abilities. When you avail yourself to God, He gives you the ability to do whatever He asks you to do.

In the natural it would appear to be in God's best interest to have Paul preach to the Jews rather than the Gentiles. Paul says of himself in Philippians 3:4-6—

> . . . though I myself have reasons for such confidence. If anyone else thinks he has reasons to put confidence in the flesh, I have more: circumcised on the eighth day, of the people of Israel, of the tribe of Benjamin, a Hebrew of Hebrews; in regard to the law, a Pharisee; as for

*zeal, persecuting the church; as for legalistic righteous-
ness, faultless.*

Even though he was a Jew, Paul had to run and hide from
the Jews because they wanted to kill him. Even though he
thought of himself faultless in legalistic righteousness, Paul
spent a good deal of his Christian life in prison.

I don't believe it was God's perfect plan for Paul to be
imprisoned; however, God wasn't going to let man or Satan
thwart His plan to reach Jews and Gentiles alike in the early
church, so He directed Paul to write what is referred to as the
Prison Letters or Prison Epistles (Ephesians, Philippians,
Colossians, and Philemon). Even prison couldn't keep Paul
from reaching out and drawing people to Christ.

What I'm trying to get across here in these examples is that
God had a purpose and a plan for each of these men, but
each one had to choose to fulfill this purpose and plan.
When we're busy fulfilling the plan God has for us, many
times the enemy will show up and try to discourage us or
harm us. God never promised the Christian walk would be
without problems. Paul says in 2 Corinthians 1:3-7—

> *Praise be to the God and Father of our Lord Jesus
> Christ, the Father of compassion and the God of all
> comfort, who comforts us in all our troubles, so that we
> can comfort those in any trouble with the comfort we
> ourselves have received from God.*
>
> *For just as the sufferings of Christ flow over into our
> lives, so also through Christ our comfort overflows.*
>
> *If we are distressed, it is for your comfort and salva-
> tion; if we are comforted, it is for your comfort, which*

produces in you patient endurance of the same suffer-ings we suffer.

And our hope for you is firm, because we know that just as you share in our sufferings, so also you share in our comfort.

Notice that Paul doesn't say "in case we run into troubles," but rather "in all our troubles." We will definitely have troubles. No one, not even Jesus, was exempt from troubles.

I don't personally know anyone who can say they've been such a threat to Satan that they had to endure anything comparable to what the Apostle Paul did. However, I would like to be a powerful enough Christian that when I wake up in the morning, the whole army of Satan begins to tremble and cry out, "Oh, noooooo, she's awake!" To be this type of Christian, however, I have to be willing to go through some stuff. Paul gives us a glimpse into his "troubles" in 2 Corinthians 11:23-27—

> *. . . I have worked much harder, been in prison more frequently, been flogged more severely, and been exposed to death again and again.*

> *Five times I received from the Jews the forty lashes minus one.*

> *Three times I was beaten with rods, once I was stoned, three times I was shipwrecked, I spent a night and a day in the open sea, I have been constantly on the move. I have been in danger from rivers, in danger from bandits, in danger from my own countrymen, in danger from Gentiles; in danger in the city, in danger in the country, in danger at sea; and in danger from false brothers.*

I have labored and toiled and have often gone without sleep; I have known hunger and thirst and have often gone without food; I have been cold and naked.

Yet Paul kept a right attitude. He didn't whine and complain that God wasn't taking care of him. He didn't ask why a loving God would allow such horrible things to happen to him. As a matter of fact, Paul says in 2 Corinthians 12:9-10 that he must be weak in order for God to be strong in him.

But he said to me, "My grace is sufficient for you, for my power is made perfect in weakness." Therefore I will boast all the more gladly about my weaknesses, so that Christ's power may rest on me.

That is why, for Christ's sake, I delight in weaknesses, in insults, in hardships, in persecutions, in difficulties. For when I am weak, then I am strong.

Even Jesus' brother, James, tells us in James 1:2-4—

Consider it pure joy, my brothers, whenever you face trials of many kinds, because you know that the testing of your faith develops perseverance.

Perseverance must finish its work so that you may be mature and complete, not lacking anything.

James also didn't say "if" you encounter trials, but "whenever" you encounter them. If Jesus had to encounter tests and trials and James and Paul had to encounter tests and trials, what makes any of us think we are exempt from them or that God is supposed to protect us from them?

Not all hardships, however, are due to being a Christian. If my electricity is turned off in the middle of the winter because I neglected to pay my bill, I cannot say that I'm suffering hardships for the Lord. I'm simply suffering hardships due to my own lack of responsibility.

In the above scriptures it's not the trial that you delight in but rather the maturing that takes place in you when you respond to that trial correctly. There will be trials! Even when the trial is the result of your own doing, take it to God in prayer and let Him teach you. A godly man or woman learns from their mistakes. A fool keeps repeating them. You can choose to become better through them or bitter because of them. All of these men had great opportunities to quit. They chose to fight the good fight of faith.

It's not just our response (physical actions) to tests and trials that affect the outcome. More often than not our actions are influenced by what we're speaking out of our own mouths and what others are speaking into our lives. My pastor once challenged the congregation to pay attention to what we were saying for 30 days. It's amazing what we discovered. We found out that we could, in fact, have what we say.

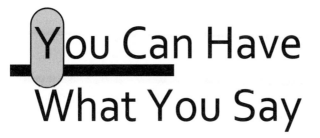

Chapter 4

You Can Have
What You Say

In Genesis we're told that man was created in the image of God and that God created everything by speaking it into existence. Genesis 1:3, 6, 9, 14, 20, and 24 say "And God said let there be . . ." All things were created by God by the power of His words.

> **Psalm 33:6**
> *By the Word of the Lord were the heavens made, their starry host by the breath of his mouth.*

> **Psalm 33:9**
> *For he spoke, and it came to be; he commanded, and it stood firm.*

> **Hebrew 11:3**
> *By faith we understand that the universe was formed at God's command, so that what is seen was not made out of what was visible.*

Does it not stand to reason then, since we were created in His image, that we too have power in our words? I heard a pastor once say that our words are powerful enough that we can talk to an incoming storm and tell it not to harm our property.

This came to mind one day as a major storm with high winds approached our city. I stepped outside and spoke to the storm and told it that it had no power to touch anything on my property. After the storm ended we went outside and found that all around us tree branches and even whole trees had been blown down. There wasn't even a tree branch in our yard! I was so excited! The next time a storm came I did the same thing, except we had an old willow tree with dead branches in it so I told the storm it could only take down the dead branches. Sure enough, after the storm was over the only damage was the two dead willow branches lying in the yard. You can dismiss this as coincidence or even suggest that I must be crazy, but I believe it was the power of my words, along with my faith, that brought about these results.

Satan also believes in the power of words, and he's very subtle with his use of them in order to trick or confuse us. One of the biggest weapons the enemy uses against us is the power of suggestion (words planted in your mind), just like he used against Eve in the Garden of Eden when he asked, "Did God really say that?"

If Satan came at us with obvious lies, he wouldn't be able to deceive us. He must come at us with a measure of truth which he very cleverly weaves deception into. His main purpose for doing this is to cause us to take our eyes off God and put them on ourselves or something else.

For this very reason we must guard our minds while reading this book to ensure we don't allow Satan to plant a thought that we are little gods. You may think that sounds preposterous but I've heard teachers proclaim from the pulpit that since we are joint heirs with Christ, that makes us "little gods." I also know of a religion that teaches once we die, if we were good enough on earth, we become gods over another planet. So Satan has already planted this ungodly thought into people's minds.

Paul warns us in 2 Corinthians 10:5 to take every thought and make it obedient to Christ. Thoughts left unguarded lead to plans which may ultimately lead to action. Godly thoughts should mature through this process as well; however, ungodly thoughts must be captured and dealt with in their infancy stage before they lead to plans. God created us with a magnificent mind, and it would benefit us greatly to understand its power.

It has been shown time and time again that the power of suggestion is a very, very powerful thing. The world calls it a psychic phenomenon. God calls it choosing life and blessings or death and curses.

I do not believe Christians should be involved in hypnosis because it opens the soul (your mind, will, and emotions) to the spiritual realm under someone else's control. The danger here is it leaves too much of a chance for the enemy to get a foothold in your mind; however, understanding how it works will help in your daily walk with God.

If you can tell someone under the power of hypnosis that an object about to be placed in their hand is a burning coal, when in fact it is an ice cube, but their hand shows the effects of a burn, then this shows the power of the mind subjected to a mere suggestion. How does this work? The body responds to what the mind says. This is simply a principle, a law that God created for our benefit. Our physical makeup is so complex and our mind so powerful that scientists have yet to figure it all out.

However, they want to take God out of the equation and say that it's a power within certain individuals. They call it mind over matter, and in a sense that's exactly what it is, but they want you to believe that it comes from the psychic realm when, in fact, it is our God-given authority in this physical realm.

The "psychic realm" is Satan's counterfeit to God's spiritual law of the power of words, and this is where we get psychics who pretend they are telling the future. Many people are drawn to these psychics to gain knowledge of their future or to have contact with a loved one who's passed on. This is very dangerous as well as forbidden by God according to Deuteronomy 18:10-12—

> *Let no one be found among you who sacrifices his son or daughter in the fire, who practices divination or sorcery, interprets omens, engages in witchcraft, or casts spells, or who is a medium or spiritist or who consults the dead.*
>
> *Anyone who does these things is detestable to the Lord.*
> ..

The psychics speak words over you and then through your fear or by you continuing to repeat these words over your life, what was spoken actually comes to pass. The Bible calls these people frauds in Ezekiel 13:6.

> *Their visions are false and their divinations a lie.*

A lot of people think they can succumb to the temptation of calling a psychic just once and there would be no harm done. James 1:14-15 tells us of the harm in such temptations—

. . . but each one is tempted when, by his own evil desire, he is dragged away and enticed.

Then, after desire has conceived, it gives birth to sin; and sin, when it is full-grown, gives birth to death.

Spoken another way: When temptation is followed by action, that action becomes sin which then leads to death (spiritual death). So rather than relying on psychics or the worldly concept of mind over matter, why not simply understand the power of words from a godly perspective and how they control many aspects of our lives. My auto accident is a prime example of this. What if I had started saying something like "Oh my gosh, I'm going to die!" when my vehicle careened out of control?

The whole incident could have been avoided in the first place had I not neglected speaking what God had instructed me to speak. Even though I gave the enemy an opportunity to take me out by neglecting these words, my words during the incident transferred the authority back to God to save me. If God was "in control" He wouldn't have required me to speak anything in the first place. He simply would have had guardian angels protect me until Satan got bored and left me alone.

My words activated the spiritual realm which gave God the authority to send guardian angels to protect me. Because we are free-will agents, it takes us working together with God in his principles to bring about blessings in our lives. Or we can speak death and curses into our lives and tie God's hands.

When we speak death and curses, it's not God who brings about the death and curse; it's sin and Satan. I hope you're able to follow me on this so far, but in case you're not, let me summarize it like this.

In God's omniscience, He knew of the enemy's plan to attack me in each of the personal stories I've shared with you, so He forewarned me of the danger and gave me instructions on how to stop the enemy's plan.

As far as the car crash, God was able to protect me from the accident altogether as long as I was speaking the words He instructed me to speak. When the words failed to come out of my mouth, this gave Satan the opportunity or the open door he needed to attack. Because I cried out to God during the attack, this again gave God authority to protect me. Had I cried out, "I'm going to die!" that is more than likely what would have happened. Remember what the police officer said? "I can't believe you walked away from that."

As for the hiking incident, God not only warned me of the impending danger, He also warned me that my continued disobedience would "tie His hands." He was definitely showing me here that I could take control of the situation away from Him and be in control of it myself, or I could listen and reap the benefits.

What God said to Moses in Deuteronomy 30:19 also applies to each and every one of us.

> *This day I call heaven and earth as witnesses against you that I have set before you life and death, blessings and curses. Now choose life . . .*

God is telling Moses that he must make a choice for himself. Either choose life and blessings or by default choose death and curses. How do we choose life and blessings? Again, Proverbs 18:21 says—

> *The tongue has the power of life and death, and those who love it will eat its fruit.*

I've heard several stories of people who actually spoke death into their lives. I do not know the names of all the people involved, but I believe the sources of these stories are genuine. I will share just a couple of them with you to help you understand just how powerful our words are.

The first story is about a man who confessed that he would more than likely be dead by the time he reached a certain age (I believe the age was 50-something). Even though he and his wife had not been taught on the power of words, the wife often told him to stop saying such things because it bothered her. He probably confessed this as often as he did more so to annoy her than because he actually believed it, but words are words whether spoken in jest or out of sincerity. Shortly after his birthday of the confessed age, he came home from work complaining his shoulders were hurting and asked for a massage. As his wife massaged his shoulders, he slumped forward in the chair and died. The autopsy showed he was in good physical condition but for "unknown reasons" his heart just stopped.

Another story involves a family of three who were involved in an auto accident. The wife and child were the more seriously injured of the three, the husband being the less injured; however, as his wife and child lay in the road waiting for an ambulance, the man kept running back and forth between them saying, "Oh my God, I'm going to die. I'm going to die." The wife and child recovered from their serious injuries, but the man died of his non-life threatening injuries. Why? The body responds to what the mind tells it and the mind believes what the mouth says.

I shared these stories with my doctor after my accident as examples in response to his question of why one person dies and another lives. What words are coming out of the mouths of either the accident victim or the doctors or family members around that person? Those words have the power of life or death whether they realize it or not, and whether they believe it or not. I truly believe we are in the position to choose life or death, blessings or curses with the words coming out of our mouths.

How many times have you heard of a doctor's report given of some sort of illness or "something" seen on an MRI, etc., but after prayer (words spoken against it) the doctor's report comes back something like this: "I don't know what happened, but it's gone." Coincidence or Christ-ordered incident because of the power of our words? I believe it is the power of our words. Let me share another story where God proved this to me personally.

Several years ago I was thinking about a $20,000 debt we owed the government. This debt was, in my opinion, a devourer of our finances. I believe in paying your debts, but this one was getting bigger and bigger due to fines and penalties that exceeded any payments we were able to make. I asked God if He would rebuke this devourer as His Word says He does for those who faithfully pay their tithes. God told me to "speak to the debt." I wasn't sure what He meant exactly so we had a little discussion (prayer). He said I had to speak to it out loud consistently until it was paid. I agreed to do this, and within a year we received a letter from this government agency stating they were closing this file and forgiving the debt. We never contacted them asking that they close the file. This was all God's influence on people and people responding to that influence, whether they were aware of it or not.

What if I had quit speaking to the debt after a month just because I hadn't seen any results yet? I believe many Christians fail to see the manifestation of their blessings because they quit speaking the blessing too soon. We want things done in our timing, not understanding what's going on in the spiritual realm. Look at what the angel of the Lord said to Daniel in Daniel 10:12-13.

> . . . *Since the first day that you set your mind to gain understanding and to humble yourself before your God, your words were heard, and I have come in response to them.*
>
> *But the prince of the Persian kingdom resisted me twenty-one days . . .*

We are unaware of the battles that take place whenever we make a request in the spiritual realm. If a request, such as the elimination of the $20,000 debt requires human involvement, then it requires all sorts of godly influence which takes time. If you don't give up, you will see the manifestation of your blessing.

Just to drive the point home, let's read some scriptures in Proverbs that tell us about the power of our words:

Proverbs 10:19-21
When words are many, sin is not absent, but he who holds his tongue is wise.

The tongue of the righteous is choice silver, but the heart of the wicked is of little value.

The lips of the righteous nourish many, but fools die for lack of judgment.

Proverbs 12:18
Reckless words pierce like a sword, but the tongue of the wise brings healing.

Proverbs 13:3
He who guards his lips guards his life, but he who speaks rashly will come to ruin.

Proverbs 21:23
He who guards his mouth and his tongue keeps himself from calamity.

Is this not exactly what happened in the previous stories? Rash speaking brings about ruin. Webster's dictionary defines the word rash as: "Marked by or proceeding from undue haste or lack of deliberation or caution."

Notice the words "lack of deliberation." In the context of the above definition, deliberation means to think about or consider, as a jury does when they go into deliberation after a trial. However, another definition of deliberation is to do something intentionally, on purpose. We can bring about blessings by deliberately choosing to speak life, and we can bring about curses by our lack of deliberation to speak life or by deliberately speaking the curse into being. We do the guarding of our tongues, not God.

Again, I want to make sure you understand that I'm not taking anything away from God by saying we're in control. God created the law of gravity. We know that if we don't have something solid under our feet, then our bodies will drop toward the earth until it finds something solid. If I walk off the edge of my deck, I'm not going to continue walking on air until I reach my destination. Once I walk off the edge

I'm going to drop to the ground. If I walk off the edge of a skyscraper, I'm going to become part of the ground! God created the law of gravity; He's in control of it in that He could change it anytime He wanted to. Until He does, however, we are in control of whether or not we respect and abide by that law. Respect it and benefit from it, or disrespect it and suffer the consequences.

In the case of our forgiven debt, I could have said speaking to a debt was stupid and I just wasn't going to do it. Had I done that we would still be paying on that debt today.

James uses great analogies in James 3:3-12 to show how powerful the tongue is. The analogy that hits home most with me is how an entire forest, sometimes hundreds or thousands of acres, can burn to the ground due to one small spark. It doesn't necessarily take much to cause great destruction. James says in verse 5 and 6—

> *Likewise, the tongue is a small part of the body . . . It corrupts the whole person, sets the whole course of his life on fire . . .*

As James says in verse 10, Christians ought to understand the power of their tongue and not allow both praise and cursing to come from the same mouth. They go to church and sing praises to God, shout Amen during the sermon, and then after service they want to gossip about Sister So-and-so. Gossip is a very destructive force. Proverbs 26:20 says—

> *Without wood a fire goes out; without gossip a quarrel dies down.*

Just as a small spark can turn into an enormous fire, destroying homes and thousands of acres of forest, gossip can spread through a church and destroy families and ultimately the church itself.

In Matthew 21:18-19 and Mark 11:22-24 we read about an incident involving Jesus and His disciples wherein Jesus shows the power of words. We read that Jesus was on His way back to the city early in the morning. Since He was hungry He approached a fig tree full of leaves, which would normally indicate fruit should be present. Upon reaching the tree, however, Jesus finds no fruit so He curses the tree by speaking to it: "May no one ever eat fruit from you again." The following morning as the disciples astonishingly discover the fig tree withered from the roots, Jesus explains in Mark 11:22-24 that with faith in God, belief in your heart, and words deliberately spoken in prayer, we can have what we say.

> *"Have faith in God," Jesus answered.*
>
> *"I tell you the truth, if anyone says to this mountain, 'Go, throw yourself into the sea,' and does not doubt in his heart but believes that what he says will happen, it will be done for him.*
>
> *Therefore I tell you, whatever you ask for in prayer, believe that you have received it, and it will be yours."*

This is the scripture used when referring to the "name it and claim it - blab it and grab it" teaching. Many people condemn this teaching because they see it as money hungry manipulation. I would agree that there have been churches and pastors who have abused this principle of God, playing on the emotional and physical needs of people to get them to give their hard earned money into a specific ministry.

That doesn't mean that every church that believes the whole Word of God and teaches that we can have what we say is money hungry. Money is not the root of all evil. The Bible tells us in 1 Timothy 6:10—

> *For the love of money is a root of all kinds of evil. Some people, eager for money, have wandered from the faith and pierced themselves with many griefs.*

It is the love of money, not money itself, that is the root of all evil. Notice that it says people eager for money have wandered from the faith. Their focus was in the wrong place.

First Timothy was written sometime between 63 to 65 years after Jesus' death. Man was falling prey to the love of money even more than 2,000 years ago. I've heard it said, "It's not wrong to have money, it's wrong to let money have you." Ecclesiastes 10:19 says—

> *. . . money is the answer for everything.*

Is the Bible contradicting itself here? Absolutely not! Try living today without money. You can't go to the grocery store and barter for your groceries with anything other than money. The only barter they'll understand is the exchange of currency based on the price they've set for the product. Again, it is the love of money that causes problems.

I heard a story once of a Christian who while driving down the road saw some money on the shoulder. He pulled over to pick the money up, but just as he reached it a gust of wind came up and blew it further down the road, so he chased after it. After this happened several more times the man looked back and saw that he had put quite a bit of distance between himself and his vehicle. He began walking back to the vehicle frustrated for his lack of success in obtaining the money. Then God spoke to him and said, "If you will quit chasing money and start chasing Me, you wouldn't be frustrated." The man got the point. When we chase God, He provides the finances we need. When we chase money, we're operating under our own power which oftentimes leads to frustration.

Just look at the current economic crisis we find our country in today. I believe it's the love of money that has put us where we are. We have businesses that are going bankrupt because their CEOs and upper management are being paid astronomical salaries. Some of these CEOs are making more money in a year than the people who actually make the business profitable (the workers) could make in a lifetime.

It's not just the CEOs who have corrupted our businesses though. There are employees at all levels who want the maximum paycheck with the maximum benefits they can get but want to do the minimum amount of work in exchange. In other words, they want something for nothing. You can't run a business with this type of mentality and expect it to survive. You can't run a country with this type of mentality and not expect it to collapse economically. The focus is on money, not on the love of mankind or the love of God.

There is no such thing as free money. When Uncle Sam bails you out, there will be strings attached called taxes that our children's children will be paying for in their lifetime. This country is suffering the effects of the love of money. We've rejected God and made money our god—we're chasing the all-mighty dollar instead of the All Mighty God.

When God and people are your focus, then God gives you blessings (wealth, jobs, health, etc.). The Bible says seek first the kingdom and then everything else will be given to you. You must seek the blessor, not the blessings.

When possessions, be it money, cars, or other things, are your focus, then you and others will get hurt. As a businessperson, your misguided focus will eventually cost the company its existence. As a Christian, your misguided focus will cause you to miss out on the blessings God has intended for you. As a pastor, you will cause a stumbling block for your congregation and cost you precious time spent with your Creator.

As a Christian, when you are willing to earn your paycheck, your focus remains on doing a good job, not on the money. The more you focus on doing a good job, the more money you will be blessed with. If money becomes the focus, the work ethic begins to decline and eventually you find yourself in an economic crisis, as our country is now experiencing.

When your focus is on things in order to show just how "blessed" you are, your focus is on you, not on God. When your focus is on creating personal fame, your focus is on you, not on God. If your focus is on things, then it can't be on God and therefore you are not hearing from Him. If your focus is on God, you will be able to hear Him properly and "things" will be given to you as needed.

But not just "as needed." God delights in prospering his people just as a father delights in giving presents to his children. Solomon, the wisest man who ever lived, and I believe that still stands today, says in Ecclesiastes 5:19—

> *Moreover, when God gives any man wealth and possessions, and enables him to enjoy them, to accept his lot and be happy in his work—this is a gift of God.*

When asked what he desired most, Solomon told God he only wanted the wisdom to rule God's people. Solomon received all the possessions—riches and wisdom—because his focus wasn't on himself or money, it was on God and leading the people with humility and honesty. Proverbs 13:21 says—

> *. . . prosperity is the reward of the righteous.*

This is the major area where God is in control. God takes care of His children, and His children are referred to as "the righteous." We are not considered righteous because of our good acts or because we obey God's commands but rather because we accept the gift of Jesus' obedience in going to the cross. When we accept Jesus Christ as our Lord and Savior we become in right standing with God and therefore become His children, not just His creation. Like the song says: "Not because of what I've done but because of who You are. Not because of who I am but because of what You've done." To be in right standing is to be righteous in God's eyes.

Let me repeat this again: The love of money is the root of all evil, not money itself, and God's principles don't just work for the Christian. A rule is a rule, and the rule is you reap what you sow. If a non-Christian pays tithes, the same principle applies to them as it does a Christian. The Bible says God causes the rain to fall on the just and the unjust alike. However, God's promises only extend to His children, not to those who reject Him. That's not to say that God brings destruction on those who reject Him, but they certainly don't have the benefit of God's protective hand or of His provisions.

Taking a couple of examples from my personal experiences, God would not have warned me about the men coming up the trail nor about speaking against the accident had I not belonged to Him. It's not that He doesn't want to help everyone but when you reject God, you are telling Him you do not want His influence in your life. God is a gentleman. He will not force His love on anyone who does not want it.

In response to that, someone might say, "Who doesn't want God's love?" You can want God's love but still reject Him by rejecting His Son, Jesus Christ, as your Lord and Savior. You reject God by saying you want to live by your own rules rather than by His rules.

When you look at countries that have rejected the one true God, you see a lot of poverty and sickness. When you live in a country whose people no longer want God's influence in their lives, you see such destruction as we in America saw on 9/11. I believe the only thing keeping America from total collapse is the remnant of true prayer warriors who worship God.

It never ceases to amaze me how selfish people can be. They tell God to leave them alone and then when something like 9/11 happens they get angry at God because He didn't protect them. You can't have it both ways. Either He's in your life or He's not!

So, how does one keep a balance between worshipping God, the blessor, and receiving His blessings, and not falling into the trap of worshipping the blessings and losing the blessor? The best way is to walk in the ways of God.

Chapter 5

Walk in His Ways

The best way to have success in life regardless of what may come your way is to walk in God's ways. Moses spoke to the Lord in Exodus 33:13 and said—

> *If you are pleased with me, teach me your ways so I may know you and continue to find favor with you.*

So, what does it mean to walk in the ways of God? I did a Bible search for the words "walk in His ways," and found a multitude of scriptures. I want to share a few of them with you. In Deuteronomy 5:33, Moses is instructed by God to teach the people the following—

> *Walk in all the way that the Lord your God has commanded you, so that you may live and prosper and prolong your days in the land that you will possess.*

In Deuteronomy 26:17 He tells them again—

> *You have declared this day that the Lord is your God and that you will walk in his ways, that you will keep his decrees, commands and laws, and that you will obey him.*

David tells Solomon in 1 Kings 2:2-3—

> *"I am about to go the way of all the earth," he said. "So be strong, show yourself a man, and observe what the Lord your God requires: Walk in his ways, and keep his decrees and commands, his laws and requirements, as written in the Law of Moses, so that you may prosper in all you do and wherever you go, . . ."*

If we were to just use the previous four scriptures, we can determine that walking in the ways of God include: One, be willing to be taught by God. For this, you must learn how to communicate with Him. Prayer and meditation are all you need to talk to God.

Two, you must learn God's laws, decrees, and requirements. The best way to accomplish this is by reading the Bible and by sitting under the teaching of a godly man or woman. Some people claim they can't read the Bible because they can't understand it. As a Christian, the Holy Spirit will help you understand what you're reading, but getting a modern day study Bible such as the NIV will also help.

Three, you must obey these laws, decrees, and requirements. It does no good to just know them if you're not going to abide by them. Once you set your heart to obey God and to walk in His ways, God will begin to give you wisdom and direction.

Isaiah 30:21 tells us that God will speak to us – we just need to learn to listen.

> *Whether you turn to the right or to the left, your ears will hear a voice behind you, saying, "This is the way; walk in it."*

Here's a personal example of how this works. I was camping with my girls once in the mountains of Colorado and we had gone for a hike. As we were returning to our campsite my oldest daughter, Angelique, wanted to take a shortcut through the trees. I didn't see anything wrong with this so I said yes. As both girls left the trail, I suddenly had a feeling there was danger lurking within the trees. My first reaction was to walk faster in order to catch up with the girls so I could protect them. But suddenly my pocket caught on a tree branch and I couldn't go any further. I turned around to pull the branch away, only to find there was no tree, no bush, nothing caught on my pocket. I knew at that moment the girls should not enter the trees. I yelled for the girls to stop and get back to me immediately! I then explained to them that God said there was danger in the trees and we were not to go that way.

I believe it was an angel who grabbed my pocket to keep me from going any further. I've often wondered what the danger was, but God has never revealed that to me. My daughters and I have always been in awe that an angel would actually physically restrain me.

You may wonder what the difference is between this encounter with God and the previous encounter on the mountain when I was hiking alone. I believe in this incident there was no time for dialogs or visions; time was of the essence. Also, God understands a mother's instinct to protect her children, just as He protects His children, so I was not acting in disobedience by racing toward my girls but rather reacting instinctively. It took a physical restraint to get my attention and make me realize that I was not to be going into the trees at all, not just to be cautious about going into them.

Whenever I hear God speak to me concerning my safety, if I listen I'm kept safe. God makes it pretty clear in Deuteronomy 30:15-16—

> *See, I set before you today life and prosperity, death and destruction.*
>
> *For I command you today to love the Lord your God, to walk in his ways, and to keep his commands, decrees and laws; then you will live and increase, and the Lord your God will bless you in the land you are entering to possess.*

It wasn't just me who was kept safe in this story but also my children. Sometimes our walk with God affects others. It never hurts to have a mother or grandmother or someone who loves you praying for you. I believe with all my heart that prayer over someone else, whether or not they are walking with God, is a very powerful tool.

As a matter of fact, I have another story which will make this point. My husband and I always pray for and over our children. When Angel was a junior in high school, she drove herself to school. One particular morning after she left at 7 o'clock, I went upstairs to the computer. At 7:15 I heard footsteps in the entryway. I didn't hear the door open nor did I hear a car outside so I thought my other daughter, Tamara, who was sleeping downstairs, must have gotten up. (Just a funny side note – my first thought was why the heck did she sleep with her shoes on?)

I went downstairs and found Angel standing in the middle of the entryway. The lights were off so I couldn't see her clearly. She asked me where the Jeep was. I didn't understand why she would ask this, so I stood there for a couple of seconds trying to figure out what was going on. She asked me again where the Jeep was, so I went to look outside in the driveway, but it wasn't there.

When I came back into the entryway, I could see her in the bathroom rinsing mud out of her mouth. At this point I realized she must have had an accident. As I was rushing her to the emergency room, I came upon the Jeep lying on its side at the bottom of a five-foot embankment, the motor still running, the back windshield shattered where the back seat had flown through it.

The Jeep was totaled and Angel had a concussion that kept her in the hospital overnight and took two weeks of her memory. But that's all! She could have been killed. Here's a picture of the Jeep after the accident.

Notice again the protection around the driver's side!!

As a matter of fact, I'll never forget how I felt the next week when there were two more rollover accidents involving teenagers who were both killed.

Although my daughter's life was spared, she did suffer the minor head injury. We spent the first six hours at the hospital with Angel thinking she "just woke up." She would look at one of us and ask what happened. We would explain that she had an accident. Then she would ask if the Jeep was totaled, to which we would answer yes. Then she would ask if anyone else was involved, to which we would answer no. She would turn her head away, sometimes starting to cry, and then look back at us and start the questioning all over again as if for the first time.

The doctor said her brain was swollen and she only had about a 20 to 30 second short-term memory span until the swelling went down. At one point Angel told the nurse that she should have come in to draw blood while "she was out." When I asked her what she meant, she said she just "came to." It was then we realized that Angel thought she was unconscious before each of these question sessions.

Her lack of injuries is proof of God's protection; however, how she got home is a real miracle. The only explanation for how she got home is divine intervention. We believe that an angel delivered her home safely. You may say that's impossible but there is no other explanation for how she could have gotten home 15 minutes after she left.

Number one, the accident occurred about five minutes down the road. Number two, being a mile and a half down the road she could not have walked that distance in ten minutes. Number three, no human in their right mind would pick up an accident victim covered in mud, repeating herself every few seconds which indicates a head injury, and just drop her off at her home without coming to the door to explain to her parents what happened.

There are other factors also, such as I didn't hear a car pull up or didn't hear the front door open, and our dog, Bear, didn't bark, which he would have been doing incessantly if there had been a strange car outside. We, as mere mortals, don't understand fully and can't always see what happens in the spiritual realm unless God reveals it to us.

If you want to read a very interesting story in the Bible that will attest to this, read 2 Kings 6:8-23. Elisha was a very godly man who operated in the spiritual realm, it seems, with much ease. He simply understood whom he served and knew the powers that were at his disposal. The story goes like this.

The king of Aram was at war with Israel. The king of Israel was depending on Elisha to keep him informed of the king of Aram's plans. Elisha didn't have a spy in the enemy's camp to gather top secret information for him. Elisha got his information from his all-knowing God. Look at verses 11 and 12. The king of Aram summoned his officers and demanded of them to tell him who was feeding information to the king of Israel. Their reply—

> *"None of us, my lord the king," said one of his officers,*
> *"but Elisha, the prophet who is in Israel, tells the king*
> *of Israel the very words you speak in your bedroom."*

Now, I'm sure the king did not conduct his wartime affairs with his generals from his bedroom. What the officer was saying here was that Elisha knew even the secrets the king of Aram had spoken.

Enraged at this information, the king of Aram decided to capture Elisha, so he sent out a party to accomplish this. Upon seeing the army surrounding the city where Elisha was, Elisha's servant became afraid. Elisha's reaction is in verses 16 and 17.

> *"Don't be afraid," the prophet answered. "Those who are with us are more than those who are with them."*
>
> *And Elisha prayed, "O Lord, open his eyes so he may see." Then the Lord opened the servant's eyes, and he looked and saw the hills full of horses and chariots of fire all around Elisha.*

Isn't that awesome! Our prayers are just as effective when we're walking with God. I believe our prayers as well as Angel's personal relationship with God saved her from death. I am so thankful that God is such an awesome God that He could use an angel of His to deliver our Angel home to us just as he used angels to watch over and protect Elisha.

Another story of God's protective hand is when our daughter, Tammy, one summer night slept outside in her clubhouse. Unbeknownst to her, I had let her dog, Bear, in the house during the night. Something woke her up at some point and she realized Bear was not in the clubhouse, but she could hear him walking around (or so she thought) in the yard. When she called him in, two dogs came into the clubhouse. She figured someone must have let our other dog, Cassie, out thus explaining the second dog. She made them lie down and she went back to sleep. The next morning when she woke up, she discovered two strange dogs in bed with her. The dogs took off running down the road, and a short while later we discovered one of our lambs had been mauled and one was missing.

The thought of two dogs who had just attacked and killed a lamb for the sheer joy of killing climbing into the clubhouse and sleeping with my daughter made me momentarily sick to my stomach. But then I realized that once again God was watching over my children.

It's not just individuals or individual families that are affected by our lifestyles. I also believe that a country is blessed or cursed by the moral character of its rulers. When reading about the many kings in the Bible, if he was a good king and found favor with God, it is recorded that he walked in the ways of God and the people were blessed and flourished. If he was a wicked king, then it was recorded that he did evil in the eyes of God or he walked in the ways of his wicked father before him and the people were often attacked by the enemy or suffered many different hardships.

So, more simply put, to walk in the ways of God is to do what is right in His eyes. When we do what is right in His eyes, be it as an individual or as a nation, we are blessed with long life and abundant provisions.

The next question then would be what is right in the eyes of God? That's actually very simple. We only need to look at the Ten Commandments to see the moral character of God, but we could also review the lives of those in the Bible who found favor with God.

I'm not going to list the Ten Commandments, but if you need to refresh your memory, you can find them listed in Exodus 20:3-17. Nor am I going to discuss every person in the Bible who found favor with God. Later in the chapter, however, I will mention just a few extraordinary men from the Bible who possessed godly character in order to show what godly character looks like.

As Christians, if we possess the same moral characteristics as God, then everything we do will be right in His eyes. First and foremost, we should not have anything in first place in our lives above God. Not money. Not sports. Not TV. Not our jobs. Not even other "godly" people.

Especially here in America it is easy to fall prey to idol worship. We even have a TV show called "American Idol." Now, I'm not saying we shouldn't watch television; nor am I saying we shouldn't recognize a person's talents. What I am saying is that if you'd rather stay home and watch TV than go to church or be involved in a humanitarian act in your community, then you have placed that TV or show as an idol in your life above God.

Another form of idol worship is when we worship the pastor or some other "godly" person in the church. This happens frequently in churches where religion is more prominent than personal relationships with God. The people begin to praise the pastor, and then that pastor loses sight of who he serves and embraces having the people serve him. One of the most disturbing examples I've ever seen of this is when I heard the pastor of a church tell the congregation that if they wanted his anointing, then they needed to bring him money. Several people immediately got up and put money on the pulpit so the pastor would pray for them. What a disgrace that is for the body of Christ!

Number one, it's not the pastor's anointing to give, it's God's. Number two, you can't buy the anointing, it's a gift. Scripture to back this up would be in Acts 8:18-21.

> *When Simon saw that the Spirit was given at the laying on of the apostles' hands, he offered them money and said, 'Give me also this ability so that everyone on whom I lay my hands may receive the Holy Spirit."*

> *Peter answered: "May your money perish with you, because you thought you could buy the gift of God with money!*
>
> *You have no part or share in this ministry, because your heart is not right before God."*

It's not wrong to give money to your pastor as a gift, but it is wrong to give it to him to "buy" his blessing or try to obtain God's anointing. The pastor is there to teach the Word of God to the congregation and to lead the congregation in whatever work God calls them to do. He is not God nor is he worthy of worship. No man died on a cross for mankind except Jesus Christ. He, and He alone, is worthy of our worship.

Have you ever heard a pastor tell his congregation that he is a "gift from God" to them? I have, and I believe that pastor was operating under a religious spirit rather than the Holy Spirit. The office of the pastor is discussed in Ephesians 4:11—

> *"It was he who gave some to be apostles, some to be prophets, some to be evangelists, and some to be pastors and teachers, to prepare God's people for works of service, so that the body of Christ may be built up until we all reach unity in the faith and in the knowledge of the Son of God and become mature, attaining to the whole measure of the fullness of Christ."*

Jesus "gave" these different offices to the church. This is why some pastors express that they are a "gift from God" to the church. Semantically they are correct, but it's the heart of a man that God looks at, and a man with a pure servant's heart would not dwell on himself being a gift but would rather see the congregation as a gift to them from God.

The above verse explains why Jesus gave these different offices, including the pastor, to the church – so that the body of Christ may be built up until we ALL reach unity in the faith.

A pastor's job according to Ephesians 4 is to prepare God's people for works of service, not create a bunch of idol worshipers who worship him. When Moses was sent to rescue God's chosen people, Moses didn't consider himself a gift from God to these people. He treated them as if they were a gift from God to him. Jesus even says in John 17:6—

> *I have revealed you to those whom you gave me out of the world. They were yours; you gave them to me . . .*

Can you see the difference in the heart attitude? Jesus was most definitely a gift from God, but His heart attitude was that He was given a gift; the disciples. Jesus was a servant of servants, and pastors should emulate this moral character and see his congregation as a gift rather than expressing to them that he is their gift.

I think every pastor should have Matthew 23 memorized, or at least to read it daily, because Jesus tells them what they should and shouldn't do as leaders in the church. I'm going to summarize it rather than print it here because it's quite long. I would, however, encourage you to get your Bible out, if you don't have it already, and follow along.

First, Jesus tells the people that they must respect and obey their spiritual leaders, but if these leaders do not display godly characteristics by practicing what they preach, then they, the people, should not imitate them. If the preacher teaches the congregation that they should be out tending to the poor, then he, himself, should be seen doing the same. If he teaches servanthood, then he should be the prime example of what a servant looks like.

Second, in verse 5 Jesus says that what these leaders do (the ones who do not display godly character), they do for the benefit of man to see. He's referring to the teachers of the law and the Pharisees, but today we could apply this to the pastors of churches. The Bible tells us in Matthew 6:1-4 that if you do "acts of righteousness" in order to be honored by men, then the honor you get from them is your full reward. You will not receive a reward from God because you were not looking to receive from Him.

Third, Jesus talks about how they, the Pharisees and Sadducees, exalt themselves above others by their clothing and how they dress in such a way to bring attention to themselves, how they like to be the guest of honor at events, and how they want to be called "Rabbi" in public.

If your desire is to be the "best dressed pastor in town," then your focus is on you and being honored by man, not on God. God doesn't look at the clothing we wear, He looks at our heart.

Today we call the leaders of our churches priests, pastors, or reverends. I don't believe Jesus is saying that this is wrong; however, if the leader of the church DEMANDS that he be called Pastor so-and-so, then he is operating in the same spirit as the men Jesus was referring to in these scriptures. You can honor your leaders by calling them Pastor so-and-so, but when the title is demanded, then the spirit of that person is to lord it over you that they are of a higher spiritual position. Going back to the beginning of Matthew 23, this is not a spirit of service but rather one of dictatorship and is not a godly character.

Jesus tells the people in verses 8 thru 10 that they're not to give themselves any title that would exalt them above others. They are to keep a humble attitude of a servant toward one another because they are all brothers, equal. Jesus summarizes it all up in verses 11 and 12—

> *The greatest among you will be your servant.*
>
> *For whoever exalts himself will be humbled, and whoever humbles himself will be exalted.*

Humility is probably the best godly characteristic a person can possess; however, the most common godly moral characteristics all Christians should strive for is truthfulness, honesty, good work ethic, and dependability.

As Christians, we should have companies seeking us out as employees because they know they can trust us and depend on us. We ought to be known as the hardest workers, honest to a fault, and the most dependable people there are. Unfortunately, the world has become so churchy and the church has become so worldly that it's hard to tell the two apart.

I think it's a disgrace to the church and to God to see a person who professes to be a Christian do as little as possible on the job or who is willing to stab their coworkers in the back for personal gain. A professing Christian ought to be the most helpful person on the team, one who does not gossip about others on the job, and one who is quick to stop others from doing the same. Our church family should see the same person in church on Sunday as they see outside the church the rest of the week. We have too many "Sunday morning Christians."

Now let's look at some men in the Bible who "walked in the ways of God." First, Abraham was called a friend of God and was chosen to be the lineage through which God would bring forth Jesus into the world. But what did he do to walk in the ways of God?

First, he was obedient. When God told Abraham to leave his county and travel to a new country, he obeyed even though he didn't know where God was taking him.

Second, he was generous; thinking of others before himself. When Abraham and his nephew, Lot, had to separate because they had each become so prosperous that the land couldn't hold both of them, Abraham gave Lot his choice of land rather than taking the best for himself and leaving what was left for Lot.

Third, Abraham had faith like no one else. Even though he waited over 20 years for his promised son and even though he was too old to be having children, when God tested Abraham by telling him to sacrifice Isaac on the altar, Abraham did not hesitate to obey. Why? Because Abraham had complete and total trust in his God. Let's read Genesis 22:3-5—

> *Early the next morning Abraham got up and saddled his donkey. He took with him two of his servants and his son Isaac. When he had cut enough wood for the burnt offering, he set out for the place God had told him about.*
>
> *On the third day Abraham looked up and saw the place in the distance.*
>
> *He said to his servants, "Stay here with the donkey while I and the boy go over there. We will worship and then we will come back to you."*

Notice he said "we" will come back to you. Abraham had no doubt he would be bringing Isaac back home with him. I'm not sure what was going through Abraham's mind as to how God was going to accomplish this, but it's clear that Abraham had enough faith in God that he was willing to meet the test.

The Bible tells us that Moses also was called a friend of God. In fact, we're told that God spoke to Moses face to face.

> **Exodus 33:10-11**
> *Whenever the people saw the pillar of cloud standing at the entrance to the tent, they all stood and worshipped, each at the entrance to his tent.*
>
> *The Lord would speak to Moses face to face, as a man speaks with his friend . .*

Wouldn't you love to have it recorded in history that you were a 'friend of God' and that you actually spoke 'face to face' with God? So what did Moses do to make himself so extraordinary? He had unfailing loyalty.

Moses had a pretty plush life living in the palace but he was loyal to his own people, the Hebrews.

> **Exodus 2:11-13**
> *One day, after Moses had grown up, he went out to where his own people were and watched them at their hard labor. He saw an Egyptian beating a Hebrew, one of his own people.*
>
> *Glancing this way and that and seeing no one, he killed the Egyptian and hid him in the sand.*

The next day he went out and saw two Hebrews fighting. He asked the one in the wrong, "Why are you hitting your fellow Hebrew?"

When I read this account of Moses, I see a man who is full of compassion and sorrow because his people were being oppressed. He could have told himself that he was no longer a Hebrew but an Egyptian and continued living the "good life." Instead, he put himself in danger to protect his people. True loyalty is when you are willing to lay down your life for that of another.

Everyone knows the story of Moses and how he led his people to freedom, but his loyalty is displayed the strongest, in my opinion, at Mount Sinai.

We read in Exodus 19 that only three months after leaving Egypt, Moses and his people arrive at Mount Sinai. Moses went up the mountain to talk to God, and we can read in chapters 19 through 31 the instructions God was giving Moses at this time to tell the people.

While Moses was talking face to face with God, the people became restless and decided they needed a god they could see. So they made a golden calf to worship. God then tells Moses to leave Him alone so He can destroy these wicked people and make Moses into a great nation. Keep in mind that Moses has endured three months of dealing with these people who just don't seem to be satisfied with anything. They've grumbled and complained about everything! But does Moses say, "Thanks, God. I think that's a wonderful idea because I'm really tired of dealing with them myself."? No, he stands in the gap between them and God's anger and talks God into changing His mind. That's loyalty.

Then there is David who was called "a man after God's own heart," and "the apple of God's eye." Wow! What I wouldn't do to have God look down and see me in this huge universe and say, "You are the apple of My eye."

What sort of things did David do to merit God's favor? First, when he was out in the field tending to his father's sheep, he didn't grumble and complain. Even though he was just a teenager, and I'm sure he would rather have been with his friends, David worshipped God through songs while he worked for his father.

When it came time for another king to be appointed, God did not choose any of David's seven older brothers but instead chose David because of his heart. Even though God had already rejected Saul as king and appointed David as his successor, David never showed anything but respect for Saul as long as he was alive. David was a hard worker, an obedient son, and most importantly he respected authority.

The last person in the Bible I want to talk about is Enoch. Unfortunately I can't tell you what he actually did to merit God's favor other than "he walked with God." In Genesis 5, we are given a condensed account of the family tree from Adam to Noah. Most of these men lived to a ripe old age of between 700 and almost 1,000 years. But notice verses 21 through 24 concerning Enoch. We are told in verse twenty-two that Enoch "walked with God." We're told again in verse 24 that Enoch "walked with God." Enoch walked in the ways of God to the point that God took him to heaven at the "young" age of 365 years.

You see, the others "lived" to be such-and-such years old; Enoch "walked with God" for such-and-such years. There's a difference between just "living for" and "walking with" God.

Walking in the ways of God is simply doing in every situation what Jesus would do. He was obedient to authority, selfless in giving of Himself, and forgiving of those who persecuted and abused Him without cause. If all mankind possessed the same moral character as Jesus did and had the fortitude to do the right thing because it was the right thing to do, not just because there were personal benefits in doing so, then we wouldn't need laws to govern us.

Jesus said that the greatest law was the law of love. If we would walk in love, we would absolutely walk in the ways of God. God loved His creation so much He was willing to die for it. Being a spirit, He could not die Himself, so He came to earth in the form of man in order to die on the cross for our sins.

The Bible tells us in John 14:6 that Jesus is the only way to heaven. If you've never accepted Jesus Christ as your Lord and Savior, then you will not be able to enter heaven upon your death. God made it very simple for all his creation to enter heaven. All you have to do is accept the gift He gave – Jesus Christ.

There are no magical words nor is there a specific prayer one must pray to be saved. All you have to do is believe that Jesus is the Son of God, that He came to this earth and died on the cross for your sins, came back to life three days later, and is now in heaven at the right hand of God. Once you believe this, the Bible says you must confess it with your mouth and then you will be saved.

What does it mean to be saved? It means to be rescued from a sentence to hell and an eternity of separation from God.

If you'd like to be saved and join the family of Christians, please make that confession now in your heart and then out loud with your mouth. Find yourself a good Spirit-filled, full gospel church and get involved in sharing the gospel with others. You will then be walking in the ways of God.

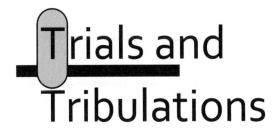

Chapter 6

Trials and
Tribulations

As I discussed in a previous chapter, when you walk in the ways of God, life doesn't become a bed of roses. As a matter of fact, sometimes all hell breaks loose, or so it seems, when you walk in His ways. Every godly character in the Bible went through some rough times, and there are no exceptions for us in this era.

I'd like to share with you now a modern day Joseph story of trials and tribulations. Only this story involves two women whom I'll call Anne and Barb.

Anne was on staff at a church and went through some personal attacks from within the church just like Joseph went through attacks from his own family. Your church should be your extended family. However, not everyone who attends church is there to serve God. Some are there to serve themselves or, in the extreme, to serve Satan. These people are called wolves in sheep's clothing. I wouldn't be surprised to find that every church has at least one of these wolves sitting anywhere from the back pew to the front pew in a position of leadership.

Anne had to endure many occasions of being falsely accused and ostracized at the hand of one such wolf named Barb in her church. To make matters worse, when Anne went to God in prayer concerning addressing this with the pastor, God told her that she was not to address Barb with the pastor because if she did the pastor would "turn against her." The pastor lacked discernment and had been deceived, as many Christians are from time to time, by this tool (person) of the enemy. He could not see that this was a wolf in sheep's clothing causing damage to his congregation.

You see, the enemy never introduces himself as the enemy nor lets you in on his plans to bring destruction into your life. He comes in like an angel of light, with all the right words in all the right places. If he came knocking on the pastor's door saying, "I'm sending in one of my wolves to cause confusion and destruction within your congregation, and I would like you to put her in a position of leadership," no pastor in his right mind would do it. Satan is very subtle and crafty, and we must be on our face before God in all things each and every day so that we can discern the plans of the enemy.

God told Anne that things would be revealed in time and that she was to simply cover this situation in prayer and walk in love. This is all well and good spiritually, but what about when the flesh rises up and wants to scream "foul!" Then you constantly go to God in prayer and ask Him to help you walk in love. The Bible says that love covers over a multitude of sins.

There was even a time when Anne began having one physical ailment after another, and one home disaster after another. Through taking authority over these ailments and situations Anne successfully beat each one but was becoming physically exhausted through the battle. One day while in prayer God informed her there was someone specifically targeting her in prayer to Satan. God told her to begin reading out loud daily Psalm 35, so she did. Even after the physical attacks stopped she continued to read this Psalm out loud for weeks. She finally felt a release in the spirit and knew that something had happened.

Here is just the first part of Psalm 35—

> *Contend, O LORD, with those who contend with me; fight against those who fight against me. Take up shield and buckler; arise and come to my aid.*

God is not a gossip, so He did not tell Anne who was praying to the enemy against her. Common sense told Anne who was praying against her; the same person who had falsely accused and ostracized her. But the "who" didn't matter as much as the words themselves being spoken, so the only way to effectively fight this foe was by the written Word of God. Jesus Himself set the example when being tempted by Satan by using the Word of God against him.

Why am I sharing this story with you? To show you that even when the enemy is within the church, if you walk in the ways of God through prayer, love, and obedience, God will always bless you. You don't know what drives a person to work for the enemy. Barb (the wolf in sheep's clothing) may have been so verbally or physically abused at home that she felt the only way to feel some semblance of power or control was to allow herself to be used by Satan.

I know a woman who is in a position of leadership at a church and is demon possessed. When I asked God how this could be, He explained to me that this person wants to serve Him but will not let go of the demon because she's convinced she controls it and only uses it when she needs to feel powerful or in control. This, of course, is a very clever deception on the part of the demon.

How then can she be in a position of leadership at the church? Again, a lack of discernment on the part of the pastor. Pastors are not perfect. They need to be bathed in prayer daily by those who are discerning.

So, how did Anne walk in the ways of God through these trials? First, she obeyed God in everything He instructed her to do; and second, she never confronted the enemy in the flesh even when she was being falsely accused and ostracized. Instead, she consistently spoke the Word of God over the situation. Because of this obedience, God promoted Anne to a position of management and increased her pay by one and a half times.

What about Barb? As God said, things will be revealed in time and she'll lose her hold on the congregation and the pastor. Actually, before this book went to print I was informed this was already happening.

Anne's prayer is that Barb would come into the fullness of God and see that the enemy only deceives and is not helping her at all but is actually hindering her walk with God.

Now I'd like to share my sister's story. I mentioned in the Dedication that Teresa died at the young age of 34. Her trials and tribulations were the result of a bad decision to get involved in drugs. In the year 2007 Teresa was but one of thousands of people who died due to drug abuse. Having never been on drugs, it's so easy for me to say that this is a senseless way to die.

Why do people get themselves hooked on drugs in the first place? I've heard many different reasons, such as peer pressure, curiosity, and for some people a way to escape the harshness of reality in their lives.

So what was Teresa's story? When I asked her why she started using drugs, she said it started with smoking marijuana sometime in her teenage years, which she felt was an innocent drug to use. But she also admitted that marijuana was a gateway to more potent and dangerous drugs.

Smoking marijuana is like playing along the edge of a cliff. After awhile you become so use to the edge being there that you gain a false sense of security. Many bad decisions are made when one harbors this false sense of security.

Teresa's bad decisions continued when she decided to try the next fad her friends introduced her to, which was inhalants. A person's choice of friends oftentimes reflects the lifestyle they themselves are living. One bad friend introduces you to another bad friend, who introduces you to another bad friend, etc. After inhalants it was on to the next level which was crack and other hard drugs.

Sometime during all the drug use Teresa also became an alcoholic. I believe the drug use started out as a teenage sense of curiosity and possibly a desire to fit in with the kids in the neighborhood. The alcohol became her escape from the shame of doing drugs and not being strong enough to stay away from them.

Teresa said she felt more confident in herself while on drugs. She felt beautiful and believed she could accomplish whatever she wanted. Of course, after the drugs wore off then she felt ashamed of herself, belittled herself for not being strong enough to stay off them, and then battled with the desire to feel good about herself again. This is the vicious circle of lies one goes through when addicted to drugs.

I believe the enemy gets involved with people who are on drugs and is partly responsible for the thought processes they struggle with. It's like when a young girl finds herself in a situation where she is contemplating having an abortion. The enemy is right there with all the reasons why the decision to abort is the best decision for all concerned, but then after the act is done, he's the first one there to scream "baby killer."

Teresa just never seemed able to free herself from this vicious circle of lies. There were times when she would fight hard to stay clean and just when she would begin to feel proud of herself for finally beating this addiction, something would happen to plunge her right back into it.

But each plunge was Teresa's own decision. No one forced her, to my knowledge, to do drugs or to drink alcohol. We all choose the way we handle situations in our own lives, and it was no different for her. It was not WHAT was going on in Teresa's life that killed her, it was her REACTION to what was going on that killed her. She reacted by using cocaine and her body reacted to the abuse by shutting down.

Chapter 7

Don't Over-
Spiritualize

Many Christians I've met over the years tend to over-spiritualize the events in their lives. Anytime something happens (usually this applies to the negative events), they want to know if it was Satan attacking them or God allowing it to happen for some unknown reason.

I don't know how many times I've heard a Christian who was hospitalized say that it was the only way God could get their attention. My response to that is, "I wouldn't want to serve a puny god like that." If the Creator of the universe has no more power to get His creation's attention than to cause him or her to be flat on their back, He's not a very powerful God. On the contrary! It's usually because we're flat on our back with nothing else to do that we take the time to listen to God.

My point is that it may not have been Satan or God who put that person in the hospital. Things simply happen in this world we live in with so much technology and the vast population of people. Just by sheer statistics, when you have as many vehicles on the road as we do today going at the speeds we go, there are going to be auto accidents. When you live in a time and place where sin prevails, there are going to be negative incidents that occur.

Man is fallible. When you have man inventing, building, and running machinery (although the knowledge of such inventions comes from God), there are bound to be accidents. When a fork-truck driver accidentally runs over a coworker's foot and crushes it, the event does not have to be attributed to Satan as the one who comes to steal, kill, and destroy; nor should the coworker believe that the accident was ordained by God since he received a huge financial settlement from the company.

Because Adam and Eve sinned in the Garden of Eden, sin is allowed to run rampant on this earth. The Bible tells us that Satan is the ruler of this earth so it would only stand to reason that sin would be all around us. Because of this sin our environment is not the cleanest, our food sometimes has chemicals in them that God never intended for us to eat, and sickness and disease are an ongoing problem.

When we put stuff into our bodies that is not supposed to be there, it creates a breeding ground for some of these diseases. If a person overeats and suddenly one day finds himself weighing over 300 pounds, did Satan do it or did God? Neither! It's the fault of the person doing the eating.

When the doctor tells an alcoholic that his liver is damaged, it's not an attack of the devil but rather an attack of the booze he's consuming. When people play Russian Roulette with their lives, they can only blame themselves. It's not right to try and lay blame anywhere else, be it Satan or God.

I do believe, however, that some diseases are actually manifestations of demons, but that's another subject altogether. I also believe that Christians do not have to get sick. We can claim our authority in the name of Jesus and command the sickness to leave our bodies. We can also listen to God concerning things we can do in the natural to keep our bodies healthy. I have experienced many times in my life when God has told me to do something in the natural in response to something going on in my body.

For example, when I moved to Michigan, I found myself fighting with allergies. When I went to God with it, He said to drink more water and consume local honey. As long as I follow this, I do not suffer at all from the allergies. Were the allergies an attack from Satan? I don't believe so. Otherwise when I rebuked it, it should have left. When it didn't, I went to God, and He showed me how I let my immune system get weak. So, between strengthening my immune system, drinking plenty of water, and using honey almost daily, I haven't had an allergy issue in a couple of years.

Why then do some Christians die of diseases such as cancer? That's a question I cannot answer. I've seen Christians healed miraculously of cancer, and I've heard of Christians dying from cancer. The only thing I can say about that is we don't know what was going on in the person's life. Going back to "you can have what you say," maybe they were speaking death rather than life over themselves. Maybe there were family members speaking death over them. Only God knows why.

We cannot fathom what is going on in the spiritual realm around us on a daily basis. I don't believe most of us could handle it if we could see what was going on. But that does not mean that everything that happens is of the spiritual realm. Sometimes life just happens. What's wonderful to know though is when life happens, no matter how big or small, God can take that situation and turn it for our good.

The example of someone being hospitalized, for instance, may not have been God's plan nor Satan's attack, but God can take that situation and reach either the person hospitalized or use that person to reach someone else in the hospital. All through life we should be asking God for the opportunity to be reached or to reach someone else. We don't know who around us may be close to entering eternity.

While writing this book we experienced two weeks of trials and tribulations that may or may not have been an attack of the enemy.

First, my husband received a phone call on Thursday saying he would be laid off from work for another week.

Second, late Friday afternoon I discovered our mortgage company had overdrawn our checking account by taking out two mortgage payments that same week. This, of course, caused over $300 in overdraft fees over the next week.

Third, while on the phone with the mortgage company on Saturday, my husband brings me a letter from our home owners insurance company that he just retrieved from the mailbox which read they were cancelling our policy because we "no longer fit their qualifications." I was on the phone almost daily for a week and a half with the mortgage company attempting to get our money back and the insurance company to ensure we continued to have coverage.

Fourth, on Tuesday, while on the phone with the mortgage company yet again, the well pump stopped working. It was determined that the existing well collapsed and was allowing sludge through the line which plugged up the pump.

Not only were we overdrawn on our checking account and therefore couldn't purchase gas to go to work, food to eat, or even a pack of gum for pleasure if we wanted it, we had to find another insurance company to cover our home, had to have a new well drilled which would cost $4000 dollars, and had to figure out where the money was going to come from since my husband was laid off.

We asked ourselves, "Is this an attack or just bad luck?" We really weren't sure. Could it be because I'm writing this book? Is the enemy afraid that people will be set free after reading it? Since I've been working on the book for over a year now, I don't think that's the case.

We really didn't think it was a specific attack from Satan at all or a test from God. However, in case it was, we determined we were going to speak positive things over each situation and became more determined we were not going to lose our joy. Remember, it's not the circumstance but your response to that circumstance that makes or breaks you.

In the end we found an insurance company to cover both our home owners and our auto insurance, and we'll be saving over $1000 dollars a year on premiums. We were able to borrow the money at a very low interest rate to pay for the well, and the mortgage company issued a check for the mortgage payment and the overdraft fees.

So whether it was an attack or just life, I believe because we spoke positive things over our situation and didn't lose our joy, even while dealing with no water for eight days, God made sure we came out on top. Of course, not only were we speaking positive, but we also spent time in prayer asking that God's hand be on each situation. God is a gentleman and only comes to your rescue when you invite Him to.

Another way we over-spiritualize is trying to become a puppet for God. A puppet has no brains and therefore does not have a free will. We, however, do have brains and a free will. We should learn how to use them!

As Christians we are to renew our minds, not remove them. Some Christians want the Holy Spirit to "lead" them in every aspect of their lives. There are things that you can decide for yourself and do not need the Holy Spirit to guide you. God doesn't care if you eat a bologna on rye or turkey on white for lunch today! Nor does He care if you wear the pink dress or the blue one, as long as they are both modest.

Now, if God tells you not to eat at a certain restaurant today, you better listen because something is going on that you're not aware of. It could be there's salmonella in the food or there could be a situation that God is protecting you from. He doesn't care whether you eat steak or a salad, unless there is a health issue going on in your body.

God certainly cares about all the little issues in life and is willing to guide us when we ask, but we're not to become so spiritual that we can't even think for ourselves anymore. As my pastor used to say, "Don't become so spiritually minded that you're no earthly good or become so earthly minded that you're no spiritual good."

I've taught my children to pray for God's help when they lose things because God does care even about the little things. My daughter lost her iguana, Robin, outside one day and asked me to help her find it. She was so upset that she couldn't calm down and hear what God was telling her. I prayed, asking God to show me where Robin was. He told me she was in the willow tree. Sure enough, there she was sunning on a branch of the willow tree. However, He left it up to us to use our brains on how to get her down.

Satan didn't take the iguana from my daughter nor did he hide it in the tree. The iguana was left unattended and she did what was natural to her–she climbed up in a tree. God created iguanas to blend into their surroundings so it wasn't easy to spot her. But because God said she was there, I looked until I was able to spot her. Our pets are our responsibility, not God's; however, He will help us with them if we ask.

When we first moved out in the country, our daughter's dog, Christine, ran into the street and was hit by a truck. Another driver who saw the accident stopped and picked her up and brought her to the house, explaining what had happened. Christine looked dead. She was not moving and did not appear to be breathing. My daughter held her in her arms and prayed to God to bring her back. Suddenly she felt a very weak pulse and pleaded for us to take her precious dog to the vet. What else can a mother and father do at this point?

We took her to the vet's office and he said she most likely would not make it, but he would do what he could. The next morning he called to say that we needed to come get her because she was up and around. He was amazed she made it through the night and said that she was apparently looking for her owner. No one will ever convince our daughter that God did not bring her beloved pet back to life.

I heard a saying once: "A person with an opinion can never convince a person with an experience." My family and I have had so many experiences with God in our lives that we'll never be convinced by others that what I've written in this book is nothing other than God's honest truth.

Conclusion

In conclusion, I want to share one last story that will demonstrate God's divine influence as well as the power of our words.

In 1993 my husband and I began looking for some land to purchase in order to fulfill a vision we believed had been given to us by God. The vision was to create a place for pastors to come get refreshed, restored, and renewed. We figured at the time we needed about 40 acres. My husband came home one day and said he found a place for sale with 1440 acres.

Our pastor, as well as many of the well-known televised pastors, was teaching a message on not limiting God. We agreed we should apply this teaching so we called the realtor, who informed us he had just closed on the property. In my spirit I heard the words, "The realtor will call back."

Sure enough, approximately six weeks later the realtor called back and said the property was back up for sale. We prayed and asked God what we should offer. The dollar amount He said was astronomical to us since I was only a staff sergeant in the Air Force and my husband was working at the church as the director of maintenance; however, in obedience we made the offer. Even though the amount was almost twice what the owner just paid six weeks earlier, he refused the offer.

At first we were confused, but then God said to us that this was the property He chose and it would be ours for the Pastors Retreat. With total confidence in God and excitement in our hearts we began to make plans, the first of which was to build a home. We wanted a three-bedroom log cabin with a picket fence around it.

We occasionally drove out to the property just to pray over it and to make our plans. On one such trip we discovered a three-bedroom log cabin with a picket fence around it. We called the realtor to find out if the property had been sold and he informed us the owners decided to build a house on the property to increase its selling appeal. We were so excited that they built exactly what we had said we wanted.

There was an old barn not too far from where they built the house that my husband wanted to put an office in for himself. My husband wanted to show a friend of his the place so he called the realtor and asked for a tour. The realtor, not knowing what my husband had wanted to do in the barn, was so excited to show him what the owners had done. Not only had they put an office in the barn but also a bathroom.

Our church put on a Living Nativity and we even had a live camel. I told Pastor Mark that once we took possession of the ranch we would keep the camel out there. My husband said we would need an oversized barn with a fenced in pasture. You can imagine our shock and excitement when on one of our trips out there we discovered an oversized barn with a huge fenced in pasture.

I can't tell you how exciting it was to watch all of these things being done, knowing that one day the land would be ours to use for God's glory. However, I am still human and still have to deal with feelings of doubt from time to time. On one such time we were taking a couple from the church out to see the property when suddenly God spoke to my spirit and said, "Remember what I told you. Don't let your heart be troubled."

My first reaction was that of confusion. Why was God saying this and what was the situation He was referring to? As we approached the property, we noticed a new fence around it and a security gate at the driveway with a mailbox across the road. I don't remember what the name on the mailbox was, but I do remember my heart climbing up into my throat and tears coming to my eyes. I then heard again, "Remember what I told you. Don't let your heart be troubled." It was then that I knew God was referring to the ranch. What was it He had told me? That this WAS the property He chose for the Pastors Retreat.

Even though we are still not in physical possession of the land and it's been 16 years since we made that first phone call, we have not given up on what God said: "This is the land I've chosen." We spoke what we wanted, and through God's influence these things have been accomplished. I'm not going to mention the owner's name, but I will tell you he's one of America's billionaires.

Isn't that just like God to use a billionaire to purchase the land and then make all the changes to it that we want so we can establish a much needed service for pastors and missionaries all over the world?

I pray this book has given you some valuable information to help transform your life. My goal was to show you how we have the power to shape our lives, not that we have control over God. Paul tells us in 2 Timothy 2:22-26—

> *Flee the evil desires of youth, and pursue righteousness, faith, love and peace, along with those who call on the Lord out of a pure heart.*
>
> *Don't have anything to do with foolish and stupid arguments, because you know they produce quarrels.*
>
> *And the Lord's servant must not quarrel; instead, he must be kind to everyone, able to teach, not resentful.*
>
> *Those who oppose him he must gently instruct, in the hope that God will grant them repentance leading them to a knowledge of the truth, and that they will come to their senses and escape from the trap of the devil, who has taken them captive to do his will.*

We must take an active role in teaching God's truth and in applying God's principles to our own lives. I'm not trying to start a quarrel with those who have been taught that everything is predestined because God is in complete control. I just feel that many people have missed out on God's blessings because they don't take an active role in their own lives. God IS ultimately in control of the universe and can do whatever He wants to do, whenever He wants to do it, and to whomever He wants to do it to. However, He has established rules of life and it's our job to learn them and live by them.

I believe it is irresponsible of us to believe that no matter what happens, God is in control and either allowed or caused the event to happen. If that's the case, how then can we blame Satan when we're under attack? To say that God is in control and then to blame Satan when things go wrong is to say that Satan can take control from God at will. To blame God when things go wrong is to ignore the fact that we are a free-will agent, and thus refuse to take responsibility for our own actions.

If we're not free-will agents but rather pawns on God's chess-board of life, then why was God upset with Cain when he killed Abel? Did Cain act upon the evil in his own heart, or did he simply do what God had foreordained him to do for some cosmic reason beyond our understanding?

Did God deceive Eve, through the serpent, because His ultimate goal was to kick her and Adam out of the Garden? Of course not! God knew this was going to happen, but it was Eve who disobeyed and allowed herself to be deceived. God had forewarned Adam and Eve of the danger of eating from the tree of the knowledge of good and evil, just as He forewarns us of impending dangers in our lives.

To say that everything is foreordained is to say that God "makes" people do things and then punishes them if the act is wrong; the ultimate punishment being eternity in hell. I've heard people say that God has already chosen whom He wants to go to heaven, and everyone else is foreordained for hell. I find that train of thought absolutely derailing!

God is a gentleman and He does not interfere in our lives without our invitation. The Bible says that God wants all of mankind to join Him in heaven and desires that not a single soul be lost to eternity in hell. If people die without having INVITED God into their life, they made the choice themselves to be forever separated from Him.

People are always yelling about their rights. They say they have the right to make the choices they want to make and nobody should impede their rights. God believes in your rights. He respects your right to choose hell over heaven. He respects your right to choose the life you want to live over the life He wants you to live.

Yet we are living in a time where people do not want to take responsibility for their actions. They play the blame game. It's everybody else's fault they did what they did. Paul tells us in 2 Timothy 4:1-4—

> *In the presence of God and of Christ Jesus, who will judge the living and the dead, and in view of his appearing and his kingdom, I give you this charge:*
>
> *Preach the Word; be prepared in season and out of season; correct, rebuke and encourage--with great patience and careful instruction.*
>
> *For the time will come when men will not put up with sound doctrine. Instead, to suit their own desires, they will gather around them a great number of teachers to say what their itching ears want to hear.*
>
> *They will turn their ears away from the truth and turn aside to myths.*

God has a wonderful plan for you and me, and if we will but speak to Him and let Him guide us in our daily walk, we will experience His many blessings. Don't seek Him for the purpose of the blessings though. Seek Him because He is the blessor and loves you with an everlasting love.

It's time to rise above your past, seek God's face, and become who He wants you to become and have what He wants you to have. Today is a new day. Determine in your heart that you will:

1) Accept Jesus Christ as your Lord and Savior, if you haven't already.

2) Realize how much control you have over your own life and take that control.

3) Watch what you say every day and in every situation. Purpose in your heart to speak life, not death; positive, not negative; and blessings, not curses.

4) Begin reading the Bible every day and ask God to show you how you can better walk in His ways.

5) Don't assume everything that happens is either an attack of the enemy or God's plan for your life, and remember that you have a brain and God wants you to use it.

May God bless you in your walk with Him.